What Others Are Saying About This Book:

Speech-recognition software and this book will allow you to graduate from the yellow pad to the computer without typing. This is true liberation for the creative author.
—Barnaby Conrad, Founder and Director,
Santa Barbara Writers Conference

Every nonfiction writer needs a roadmap. Whether you are keyboarding or dictating, this book will guide your way.
—Michael Larsen,
Larsen-Pomada Literary Agency

Every professional speaker needs to write a book for increased credibility and a passive-income source that keeps on giving. Dan's system is tailor-made for road-warrior speakers who can't seem to find the time to write.
—Terry Paulson, Ph.D., 98-99 President,
National Speakers Association

Busy people have trouble finding time to write. Savvy authors do several things at the same time. Dan Poynter shows you how.
—Hannelore Hahn, Founder and Executive Director,
International Women's Writing Guild

If I'd had this approach to writing when I was writing ads for electronic products and BluBlocker sunglasses my life would have been a lot easier.
—Joe Sugarman, President,
JS&A/BluBlocker Corporation

There are many ways to be rich: having a family, doing good, being recognized and even earning money. Writing books and speaking professionally are two of the best ways to get there.
—Dottie Walters, Co-author,
Speak and Grow Rich

Write & Grow Rich

Using Speech Recognition to Dictate Your How-to Book

Dan Poynter

First Edition

Para Publishing, Santa Barbara, California

Write & Grow Rich

Dan Poynter

Published by: ▞▞▚▜
Para Publishing
Post Office Box 8206
Santa Barbara, CA 93118-8206, U.S.A.
info@ParaPublishing.com
http://www.ParaPublishing.com

Library of Congress Cataloging-in-Publication Data

Poynter, Dan.
    Write & grow rich : using speech recognition to dictate your how-to-book / 1st ed.
        p.   cm.
    Includes bibliographical references and index.
    ISBN 1-56860-058-5
    1. Authorship.   2. Automatic speech recognition.   I. Title.
PN147.P665   1999   98-29873
808'.02—dc21   CIP

Contents

Chapter One 11
What Your Book Will Do
for You

Chapter Two 27
What to Write
Selecting Your Subject

Chapter Three 37
Researching Your Topic and
Checking for Competition

Chapter Four 45
Your Book's Title
and Subtitle

Chapter Five 53
Your Book's Covers

Chapter Six 73
Getting Organized
Setting Up Your Binder

Chapter Seven 87
Your Writing System

Chapter Eight 107
If You Can Speak It, You
Just Wrote It

Chapter Nine 117
Your Publishing Choices.
Selling to a Publisher or
Publishing Yourself.

Chapter Ten 131
Finding a Publisher
Finding an Agent

Afterword 141

Appendix
Resources 143
Index 163

About the Author

Dan Poynter fell into writing. He spent eight years researching a labor of love. Realizing no publisher would be interested in a technical treatise on the parachute, he went directly to a printer and "self-published." Orders poured in and he suddenly found he was a publisher too. Since 1969, he has written 74  books, 47 special reports, 500 magazine articles, 9 audiotapes and two videotapes. Most of these information products focus on book writing and publishing. In the publishing field, he is widely known for his best selling *The Self-Publishing Manual, How To Write, Print & Sell Your Own Book.*

Dan Poynter's seminars have been featured on CNN, his books have been pictured in *The Wall Street Journal*, and his story has been told in *U.S. News & World Report.* The media comes to him because he is the leading authority on nonfiction book writing, publishing and promoting.

Dan believes in using the most innovative equipment and has always been on the leading edge of technology. He wrote the first book on word processors and published the first laser-typeset book. He was the first to send a galley to *Publishers Weekly* electronically and he pioneered fax-on-demand to sell reports.

A consultant to the book industry, he was recently presented with the Benjamin Franklin Award for Lifetime Achievement by the Publishers Marketing Association. Dan is a past vice-president of the PMA.

Dan is a frequent speaker at the Santa Barbara Writers Conference, the Maui Writers Conference and many other industry events. Dan runs his own publishing company, Para Publishing, in Santa Barbara.

Foreword

The book writing and publishing industries are in a state of accelerating evolutionary change. Publishing companies are growing and consolidating; emerging technologies are transporting information at light speed; the reservoir of text is growing ever larger and the thirst for information is enormous.

The need for determined research and superior writing has never been greater. These industries require new ideas, new methods and new energies.

At the annual Maui Writers Conference, we have managed to bring writers, editors, agents and publishers together in an historic conspiracy to produce better books. Never before have these disparate groups worked together as they do in Maui (and then all year around).

Dan Poynter has subscribed to this new writing/ publishing paradigm for years and now he reveals it to you in this book. When it comes to nonfiction, Dan is the top coach for writing, publishing and, most importantly, promoting.

Read this book now; start on your book today, and I look forward to seeing you in Maui.

John Tullius
Founder and Director,
Maui Writers Conference

Acknowledgment

I have not attempted to cite in the text all the authorities and sources consulted in the preparation of this book. To do so would require more space than is available. The list would include departments of the federal government, libraries, industrial institutions, Web sources and many individuals.

Valuable information (and inspiration) were contributed by Charles "Stretch" Harris, Esq., Susan Fulton, Dr. Bud Banis, Robin Kinkead, Stacy Peña of IBM Media Relations, Ruth Rose, Charles Kent, Esq., and Joel Gould of Dragon Systems.

Karen Stedman of PenMark did the content and copy editing; Robert Howard provided another great cover design, and Christine Nolt of Cirrus Design is responsible for the typesetting.

I sincerely thank all these fine people, and I know they are proud of their contributions to the book community as well as to this work.

A Word from the Author

Thank you for investing your time and money to allow me to share this new book-writing concept with you. I will make sure your time and money are well invested.

I love books, publishing, and publishers. Unlike other industries, publishers are helpful, friendly and supportive. The reason is that no two nonfiction books are alike. It is a rarity that two books on the same subject are published in the same year. Consequently, publishers do not feel threatened by other publishers. In fact, publishers often promote other books and each other.

My system works. In the back of *The Self-Publishing Manual*, I ask readers to send me their books once they publish. I receive 15 to 20 books each week.

People can be divided into three groups:
Those who *make* things happen
Those who *watch* things happen and
Those who *wonder* what happened

Authors *make* things happen.
Start making things happen today.

Disclaimer

This book is designed to provide information about the subject matter covered. It is sold with the understanding that the publisher and authors are not engaged in rendering legal, accounting or other professional services. If legal or other expert assistance is required, the services of a competent professional should be sought.

It is not the purpose of this manual to reprint all the information that is otherwise available to authors and other creative people but to complement, amplify and supplement other texts. For more information, see the many references in the Appendix.

Book writing is not a get-rich-quick scheme. Anyone who decides to write a book must expect to invest a lot of time and effort without any guarantee of success. Books do not write themselves and they do not sell by themselves. People write and promote books.

Every effort has been made to make this book as complete and as accurate as possible. However, there may be mistakes both typographical and in content. Therefore, this text should be used only as a general guide and not as the ultimate source of writing and publishing information. Furthermore, this manual contains information on writing and publishing only up to the printing date.

The purpose of this manual is to educate and entertain. The authors and Para Publishing shall have neither liability nor responsibility to any person or entity with respect to any loss or damage caused or alleged to be caused directly or indirectly by the information contained in this book.

If you do not wish to be bound by the above, you may return this book to the publisher for a full refund.

Chapter One

What Your Book Will Do For You

Would you like to be recognized as someone who knows what he or she is talking about? Be someone worth listening to? Would you like to get paid for what you know? Would you like a job that is stimulating, interesting and challenging—a job you look forward to? Can you imagine doing what you love and loving what you do?

There are many justifications for writing a nonfiction book. Some are fame, fortune, to help other people and because you have a personal mission. Let's take a look at each of these reasons.

Fame

Imagine being a published author. Picture people coming up to you at a meeting with a copy of your book and requesting an autograph. Visualize passing a bookstore and seeing your book in the window. Consider being interviewed for an article. Imagine the fame that comes with being published.

"The author is the author-ity." —Joe Vitale, *CyberWriting*

A book provides you with more credibility than anything

else you can do: more credibility than an audiotape, a videotape, a seminar, a screenplay or a song. People place a higher value on a book than on a tape—even though the same amount of work may have gone into the production. The fact is authors are highly valued in our society.

"Recognition is everything you write for; it's much more than money. You want your books to be valued. It's the basic aspiration of the serious writer."
—William Kennedy

People think if you wrote a book, you know something. And you probably do. When you think about it, you are writing your book from the very best research plus personal experience. You research every book and article, distill them down to the essentials, direct your writing toward a specific audience and illustrate it with your personal experiences. You are earning an advanced degree in the subject. Your book validates your expertise and lends more credibility to what you say.

Dan Poynter serves as an expert witness in skydiving cases. He is not a lawyer or an engineer and yet he advises attorneys, judges and juries what happened (or what should have happened) in parachute mishaps. His eight technical books on parachutes and popular books on skydiving give him the credibility to be hired and the credibility to be believed.

"Writing ranks among the top 10 percent of professions in terms of prestige."
—Jean Strouse, *Newsweek*

More business. A book makes you stand out. An author speaks with authority. A book brings customers to your door. Writing your book can be the cornerstone for a rewarding and successful future.

"Your book is your best business card. People do not throw out books, they put them on their shelf."

Once your book is published and you become an authority, your value and opportunities increase. You can charge more for seminars, articles, speeches and consulting. Imagine the credibility and recognition your book will bring you.

Fortune

Your book will be a new profit center. There is money to be made in books.

> It was a long flight home from the Maui Writers Conference and the guy in the next seat struck up a conversation. He finally got around to "And what do you do?" I sat up proudly and announced "I'm a writer." "No, no," he quickly replied, "what do you do for a living?"

There are some starving writers out there but most of them are working on fiction, entertainment that is more difficult to sell. If you write nonfiction, put it in book form and publish it yourself, you can do very well. Many people are working on their own schedule, giving the world a piece of their mind and getting paid for it.

How much? But what does it cost to publish a book? That is like asking how much is a car? All books are different. But if you are planning to publish yourself and if you want to print 3,000 copies of a 224-page, 5.5 x 8.5 softcover book with a few photographs, black ink on white paper with a four-color cover, your printing and trucking bill will run less than $1.85 each. Then there is editing, typesetting that most of us can do on our computers with laser printers, book cover design and other pre-press expenses. After the book is printed, it has to be promoted with book reviews, news releases and some direct mail advertising. For a book like the one described here, you should budget about $10,000 to get started. A good portion of that money will be spent on promoting the book after it is printed.

> **"Many first-time authors are not concerned about the money, they want the notoriety. They get smarter on their second book and look for the money."**

That $1.85 book could sell for $14.95 or $19.95 depending upon the audience. With this spread, you won't even mind giving the bookstore or other quantity buyer a 40 percent discount.

> **"Write out of love, write out of instinct, write out of reason . . . But always for money."**
> **—Louis Untermeyer**

But what if you want to produce something more substantial? What if you want a hardcover book? Perhaps it has 224 pages and you want 3,000 copies. They will cost about $3.00 each. Hardcover business books are going for $29.95 or $34.95. Not a bad markup.

Hardcover or soft? Most smaller publishers today produce softcover books to keep costs down and achieve maximum distribution. But if your goal is to use your book as an introduction to your work, consider hardcover. Hardcover is still considered to be newer, fresher and more credible. Splitting the run between hard and softcover often costs more than putting hard covers the entire run. So, choose one or the other.

On the other hand, if you decide to sell out to a publisher, you will get an advance against a royalty rather than invest your own funds. The details will be described later.

Personal mission

Imagine being able to get the word out on something you feel strongly about.

Dan Poynter loves skydiving. He wants to share it with the world; he wants everyone to jump out of an airplane. Of course, he wants you to make safe and enjoyable jumps so you will take up the sport, join the club, buy equipment and maybe even purchase some of his skydiving books.

Since 1962, Dan has made over 1,200 jumps. He has all the highest licenses and ratings and 12 hours of time (cumulative) in freefall. He is past chairman of the board of the U.S. Parachute Association and past president of the Parachute Industry Association.

> "Certain books have exerted a profound influence on history, culture, civilization and scientific thought throughout recorded time."
> —**Robert B. Downs**, *Books That Changed The World*

When you have a sense of personal mission, your profit center is your passion center. Your vocation and avocation are the same. Why split your energies? Take a stand. Be passionate. Do not be afraid to stir up controversy. Imagine sharing your enthusiasm with the rest of the world.

Helping others

Imagine helping others with a how-to book. Your years of experience could benefit a lot of people.

"We are all wounded. Our wounds are the single greatest source of material. Bad experiences make us experts on the subject. Talk about what worked for you. You have been there." —Dr. Susan Forward

Mindy Bingham was the executive director of the Girls Club of Santa Barbara. She realized that one-on-one, she could help dozens of girls each day. But, if she took what she knew, added what she had learned, pulled documents from her files and did some more research, she could multiply her efforts and reach thousands. *Choices: A Teen Woman's Journal for Self-awareness and Personal Planning* has sold over a million copies so far.

"Words still offer the most complete kind of understanding, and they last."
—Bob Woodward, journalist/author

Imagine the satisfaction you will feel by helping many other people.

"Chase the passion not the profit."
—Terri Lonier, *Working Solo*

So you may be driven by fame, fortune, personal mission or helping other people. If you are driven by fame, personal mission or helping others, the money will follow.

"I do not think that most writers write for money alone. Good ones write mainly to please themselves and hope at the same time to please as many other people as possible." —Merle Miller

Here are four principles of financial success:

1. There is more money in selling product than hours.

Most people sell their time; they are trading hours for dollars. Some people, such as doctors, charge a lot for their time, but they are still hourly workers. There are just so many hours a day and then you have nothing more to sell. A product, on the other hand, is always working for you. It earns money even when you aren't on the clock.

> Brian Tracy is a well-known professional speaker who commands in the range of $15,000 per presentation. But these speeches also require a great deal of customized preparation time and lots of distant travel. For this reason, he has committed considerable time, energy and money to develop audiotapes, videotapes and books that are sold through a variety of distribution channels. His goal is to achieve a 20:1 ratio of product to speaking.

2. There is more money selling information about a product or service than there is in the product or service. If you have ever attended a real estate seminar, you probably noticed the speaker was selling a book in the back of the room (BOR). What is ironic is that he probably made more money on the seminar and book than on real estate. And, once published, he became a lot more famous than he was selling real estate. In fact, you probably would not have attended the seminar if he did not have the fame the book brought him.

> **"If you're creating and selling information, you'll never go out of business." —Michael LeBeouf, Ph.D.**

As a result, you bought the wrong book. You did not need a book on real estate; you needed a book on how to write a book.

Dan Poynter wrote the first book on hang gliding in 1973. Since he had a product for the industry, he attended meetings of the Hang Glider Manufacturers Association. One manufacturer observed that Dan was making more money than those who were bolting Dacron™ and aluminum together.

"Books are the main source of our knowledge, our reservoir of faith, memory, wisdom, morality, poetry, philosophy, history and science."
—Daniel J. Boorstin, Librarian of Congress

3. Books reach more people. You can only help so many people one-on-one with seminars, speeches and private consulting. Books are the most cost-effective way to multiply your efforts.

"Books are the carriers of civilization."
—Barbara Tuchman, historian

4. A book is the ideal product because it is quick, fairly inexpensive and easy to manufacture. You can produce a lot more books just by letting the printing press run.

The benefits of being an author. Authors have many advantages over those who do not write. Advanced communications allow the published author to live anywhere. All you need is access to some telephone lines and the Postal Service (so you may live anywhere with a ZIP code from Guam to the Virgin Islands.) Now you may reside where you like to vacation. While writing books requires organization and discipline, your schedule is up to you. You may drop anything at a moment's notice and travel when a good business opportunity arises. Best of all, this travel, your electronic toys and other expenses are deductible.

Dan Poynter has been able to deduct his parachute jumps, flying lessons, and aircraft rental. He has traveled to more than 40 countries and has even skydived into the North Pole.

Remember too, you may write anything you wish. Freedom of expression is guaranteed to you by the First Amendment of the Constitution of the United States. You do not have to register, get a license, or ask permission from anyone.

> "Books are a form of immortality. The words of men whose bodies are dust still live in their books."
> —Wilfred A. Peterson, *The Art of Living by Day*

Radio/TV Interviews. Everyday, more than 10,200 guests appear on some 4,250 local news, interview and talk shows across the U.S. And, about 95 percent of the guests do not have recognizable names.

Radio and television talk shows need interesting guests to attract listeners and viewers. Most people think that authors are experts and celebrities, so most of the guests booked on these shows are authors. Your book is actually your entrée to the airwaves.

Advertising products on the air is expensive, and since people are skeptical of advertising they tune it out. Interviews, however, are *editorial* matter. People listen to editorial matter. Interviews are more effective than advertising and they are free. They can be an inexpensive way to sell books.

> "Many people love to go on radio and television. In fact, I think some people write books just to get on the air."

Autograph parties or book signings are a form of product promotion not open to producers of other goods or services. Bookstores, both chain and independent, are staging events to draw potential customers into their stores. Authors are the draw.

> **"Do seminars, not signings. Attract buyers to your autograph parties." — Terri Lonier, *Working Solo***

Never do an autographing; always offer a mini seminar. An autograph party says "Come and appreciate me and buy a book"; a seminar says "Come and you will receive some benefit (information)." Always think of the *benefit* to the potential customers. How can you lure them out of the house and into the store?

Patricia Bragg, Ph.D. (Health-Science) publishes health and fitness books. To promote her mini seminar at the Earthling Bookshop in Santa Barbara, she posted handbills in all the local health food stores. Then she made a postcard mailing to her customer list within a 50-mile radius. The store was packed and she held her audience for over four hours—until closing time.

> **"For successful people, autographing scraps of paper for adoring fans is a duty. For authors, autographing (sold) books is money in the bank."**

These mini seminars may lead to more seminars or even a series of them for other groups at other locations.

Hazards of being an author. Your life changes once you become a published author. Authors are treated differently. Your status changes from that of a private person, the writer, to a public person, the authority. Some authors thrive on notoriety while others are reclusive and uncomfortable with it. If you treasure your privacy, your book will become a love-hate object.

You may discover that the public thinks you are smarter than you really are. They will seek your advice. Many people will just want to be near you. Some may even stalk you.

Writing your book is not the end of your involvement. When readers have questions, authors have a responsibility to answer the mail and respond by telephone. Use these opportunities to gather material for the book's revision. Maybe you were not clear enough or perhaps the caller is interested in an important area you did not cover.

Your friends may also treat you differently once you have published a book. Some will be happy for you and supportive while others will be jealous because they didn't write the book. People new in your field will treat you like an idol, while some of your peers will feel threatened and may be rather unkind.

The difference between a blowhard and an author is that one has taken the time to put his views on paper. Both are telling you what is good for you—how to run your life. But one is a loud mouth you avoid at parties while the other is a gifted visionary you pay good money to read. The irony is that people may not want to hear what is good for them at the social function but they will pay you $20 for the same information in a book.

"Books through the ages have earned humanity's high regard as semi-sacred objects."
—Richard Kluger, author/editor

How long will this project take? Good book writing

requires organization, discipline, and applying the seat of the pants to the seat of the chair. However, by using the organizational plan outlined in this book, your writing process will be accelerated.

Terry Paulson, president of the National Speakers Association, wrote the first draft of *50 Tips To Speak Like A Pro!* (Crisp Publications) speed typing during two long airline flights using his laptop computer. Although it's a modest publication of just over 50 pages and many of the quotations and other material already resided in existing articles in his computer, this is still a good example of speed writing.

Rick Evans wrote the 87-page *The Christmas Box* in six weeks. He published it and promoted it himself. It hit the top of the *Publishers Weekly* bestseller list and was translated into 13 Languages. He sold out to Simon & Schuster for $4.2 million.

Years ago Dan Poynter wrote the 168-page *Computer Selection Guide* in 21 days. Well, actually it took 28 days but he carefully logged the time and found that during those 28 days he did 21 days of work on the book. Some of the material was adapted from an earlier work titled *Word Processors and Information Processing*.

Dan Poynter first drafted the book you are reading in less than a week. He was able to do this by using the step-by-step system outlined in this book, speech recognition software, some of his speech notes and pieces of previously written reports.

Dianna Booher raises the bar even higher. She knocked out a 402-page book, *Communicate with Confidence* (McGraw-Hill), in 22 days. *Get a Life* (McGraw-Hill) was first drafted over a long five-day weekend and *Would You Put That in Writing* (Facts on File) took her four days.

As you follow the plan in this book, you will assemble your materials and quantify the project. If you have done some writing, or have recorded presentations that may be transcribed to writing, the whole process will be shortened.

To be realistic, your first book might take several weeks for organizing: gathering materials, setting up the binder, making the piles and doing the research. The first draft could take a week or two if you can set aside the time to marathon-write it. (We will discuss the drafts in more detail later.) The second draft requires more research and could take several weeks. The third draft is *peer review* and could take as long as three weeks. The fourth draft is the copy edit that you will probably farm out to a wordsmith. Meanwhile, you will be gathering quotations and stories, fact checking statements and figures and soliciting endorsements and testimonials.

The hardest part for most authors is the first draft—getting the bulk of the material onto disk. Peer review, for example, might take three weeks but there is very little writing here. You are simply sending out chapters and waiting for their return.

Book writing is an interesting and fun trip. It is a mind-expanding learning experience that will make you a more interesting person. Approach the project as an adventure not a chore.

> On the other hand, *The Parachute Manual*, Dan Poynter's first book, took him eight years and *The Expert Witness Handbook* took six months because he enjoyed working on it so much.

Your future is up to you. Do not just hope for a bright future. Make a decision. Plan now and soon you will be doing what you want to do. Your book will be the cornerstone for the future you are building.

There is a difference between being an *author* and being a *writer*. As an expert in your field, you have the potential to be an author. Whether you have the talent, training, inclination or time to write is not important. Since you have the information to contribute to the project, you can always hire a writer to make your material interesting to read. Few politicians and movie stars have time to write, yet many of these celebrities are published authors. Most of them have contributed the information for their books through rough drafts, dictation or interviews, but few are responsible for their entire manuscript.

Do not make excuses about lacking time. In these pages, I will show you how to do two things at the same time.

Remember that writing is a solitary endeavor so your book and your life are up to you and only you.

Chapter Two

What to Write
Selecting a Subject

Fiction v. nonfiction. In selecting a subject, we must first make a distinction between fiction and nonfiction. Fiction is entertainment and as such, it must compete for peoples' time. Other books, seeing a movie, playing with the kids—all are just a small part of the competition. Nonfiction, on the other hand is valuable information that people buy in order to save time or money. One nonfiction book does not compete with any other book. Each nonfiction book is unique.

> People are very short of time today. You can see them on the freeway trying to save time by driving, eating and talking on the carphone—all at the same time.

This book concentrates on writing nonfiction: valuable information on how to do things.

> **"Fiction writers tend to be creative, interesting people who are fun at parties.**
> **But nonfiction writers drive better cars."**

Most publishers will urge you to work on your nonfiction first and to save your fiction until you can afford it.

> Dan Poynter never knows what book he will write next; he does not plan ahead. An article, a few words from a friend or an activity may trigger an idea. He visualizes the book (and its market) and makes a decision.

"The best time for planning a book is while you're doing the dishes." —Agatha Christie.

Selecting your subject with the Six Musts. Use the following criteria to qualify your project. If you have already written the manuscript, go back and make sure it meets all six of them. Unfortunately, many authors write before considering the six musts and then they discover there aren't any potential buyers for their book.

1. The subject must be interesting to you. Write what you know. Think about what you plan to be doing in three years. What are your interests? Plan your future and your book now.

"I write to find out." —Bill Manchester.

Do not write a book on "last year's subject," one that you are no longer interested in and do not want to pursue. For example, let's say you have been selling cars for the past ten years but your hobby is golf and you are pretty good at the game. Do not write on buying cars, write it on some aspect of golf. Once your book is published, people may request interviews, articles, seminars and consulting. Plan now to make sure they approach you on a subject you are passionate about. As the poet Robert Frost said, you will be much happier if your avocation and vocation are the same.

Ask yourself: Is this really the subject I want to focus on?

2. You must have expertise or experience. You do not have to have an advanced degree; you do not need a Ph.D. But you do need personal experience, dedication to do research and a deep desire to spread the word. The most important question is "Have you been there?"

> And then he asked, "What is the hot subject right now?"
>
> I replied with a question, "what have you been doing for the past several years?"
>
> "Real estate, and I am sick of it. So what subject is selling?"
>
> "Oh, so you want to write something that will bring in a lot of money."
>
> "Yes"
>
> "OK, here it is: you want to write ransom notes."
>
> And with ransom notes, you do not even have to be good at spelling. All the words are pre-spelled for you.

A fresh outlook can be an asset. When you are beginning in a new field, you have the same questions your readers will have. Write as you learn and record as you study. Then run your manuscript by more senior people to make sure you have not left anything out or written something you misunderstood. This process, called "peer review," will be covered in the writing chapter.

> Dan Poynter became interested in the new sport of hang gliding in 1973. Being book oriented, he visited the bookstores and the library. Unable to find a book on the

> subject, he wrote one as he learned to fly. He sent finished chapters to instructors and manufacturers for review. This first book on the sport sold so well, he was able to move from New England, back to California, and buy a home in Santa Barbara.

You have to have the experience to write a good book, so please do not write a book on how to get rich unless you are already rich.

Ask yourself: Do I know what I am talking about?

3. The subject must be of interest to others. The book has to contain information people want to know or they will not buy it. Will a number of people be willing to part with a twenty-dollar bill to lay their hands on this book? Will it sell?

> **"Everything in this world has turned into show business. Politics is show business. Running Chrysler is show business . . . Sports is show business, and Henry Kissinger is show business . . . And if you're not in show business, you're really off-Broadway."**
> **—Felix Rohaytn, investment banker**

Ask yourself: If I build it, will they come?

4. The subject should be tightly focused. We live in an age of increasing specialization. Years ago, we had general, weekly magazines, periodicals such as *Colliers, Look* and *Saturday Evening Post.* They are gone now because people do not have time for or want a general magazine. Today, they read *Writer's Digest, Publishers Weekly, Graphic Arts Monthly* and *Parachutist* magazine. Target your information, your message and your audience. Narrower is better.

Marilyn Grams attended one of our first book promotion workshops. She is a medical doctor; she had recently given birth to her second child and she had just finished her manuscript on breastfeeding. Mindy Bingham asked her who her intended reading audience might be. Marilyn thought the answer was rather obvious: any woman who had given birth or who was about to give birth that is interested in breastfeeding. Mindy reminded Marilyn that she had developed a system whereby a woman could breastfeed and return to work. She suggested the book be titled *Breastfeeding for Working Mothers*. Marilyn did not want to limit her market; she wanted to sell to all new mothers. Mindy said, "Let's pretend we are in a bookstore looking for a breastfeeding book. There are eight book on the subject." Then Mindy, who has a mind like a steel trap and has never forgotten a statistic she has ever read said, "Marilyn do you know that 55 percent of the women who give birth, return to the workforce within one year?" That means that 55 percent of the potential buyers will identify with *Breastfeeding Success for Working Mothers* and the other 45 percent will spread their buying over eight books. So by narrowing the focus of the book, more buyers will identify with and purchase it.

Incidentally, women purchase 78 percent of all trade books. Aim your book at women and the majority of buyers will *identify* with it.

In just nine months in the stores, *Chicken Soup for the Teenage Soul* sold over 3-million copies; more than the original *Chicken Soup* book sold in three years.

Ask yourself: is this subject narrow enough?

5. The market must be easy to reach. Who are your

readers and where are they? You must be able to *identify* them and *locate* them. Remember that your answers are not book readers in bookstores.

Go into a bookstore on any given day. How many of the customers do you suppose are interested in a skydiving book? Not many. What is the profile of the typical bookstore browser? It is the "recreational reader," someone used to plunking down $24.95 for hardcover fiction. But check out a parachute shop. How many customers are interested in skydiving? Now the gears are turning. Where can we find a high concentration of our particular customer? What type of stores do our potential customers frequent? What magazines to they read? What associations do they join and what events do they attend? Go where the customers are.

For example, skydiving books are sold through parachute stores, skydiving catalogs, skydiving schools and to the U.S. Parachute Association for resale to its members. Reaching buyers is easy and inexpensive. These dealers purchase by the carton, feel a 40 percent discount is generous, pay in 30 days and never return a book. Bookstores, in contrast, buy two or three books, complain about the discount, might pay in 90 or 120 days and then return one book for a refund. And often it is damaged.

"Bookstores are a lousy place to sell books."

Ask yourself: Do I know where my potential customers are?

6. The market must be large enough (but not too large). The primary group you are targeting should be between 200,000 and 700,000 identifiable and reachable people. To get these numbers check the membership of applicable associations, the subscriber count of appropriate periodicals and the turnout for events they might attend. If the group is too small, you won't sell enough books to quit your day job. If it is too large, you will have competition. In large groups, you will have to narrow your target even more. For example, there may be ten-million water skiers. How about a book aimed at water-ski instructors?

"You are not just an author, publisher, publicist, speaker or consultant. You are an information provider."

Eventually, you will want a line of books, tapes, disks, seminars and speeches, all covering the same subject. These products and services will fill up your brochure. Then you will become known as the source for all information on your subject.

Your book is the foundation for your business. The other products and services are built on top of the book. The book must come first as it provides more credibility than any other product. Don't spend time making an audiotape just because you can turn it out faster. Do the book first. Ask yourself: Is my projected audience large enough to support me?

"If it doesn't work, begin something else."
—Bernard Malamud

If you satisfy the six musts, you are on your way.

Stay in one field. Once you select your subject, stick to it; stay in one field. Many authors write a book on a subject they know quite well and direct it to their own (reachable) field. The book becomes a success using this formula and they suddenly think selling books is easy, so they write a travel book. It flops because they do not know how to reach the travel-book buyer.

Dan Poynter has written 74 books on ten different subjects. He found that he could not keep up; he could not maintain an expertise in all fields. He could not even read all the free magazines he received. In desperation to maintain credibility with his readers, he cut back to three: book promotion, skydiving and expert witness—and it is still too much.

One day, Dan Poynter received a call from a customer. He said "I am a chiropractor and I recognize that while chiropractors are good at what they do, they are not good at running their offices. But I have solved that challenge. I have just finished my book titled *How to Run Your Chiropractic Office.*

"Sounds good," said Dan. He thought to himself: "now here is an author who can look into the mirror and see a reflection of his customer. He knows who the customer is, what the customer needs and (most importantly) where the customer is."

Then the doctor continued with "I have a packaging idea I would like to run past you." Dan leaned back in his chair and listened. "once I sell this book to all the chiropractors, I think I'll go through the manuscript with search & replace and change the word "chiropractor" to "dentist" and sell the same book to all the dentists. Next, I'll sell to all the medical doctors. Isn't that a great plan?"

"No," said Dan, "It sounds great, but it is a terrible idea. First off, it will not be all that easy to sell to your peers. It will take reviews in your magazines, displays at your conventions, lots of mail and telephone calls. Finally word-of-mouth from one doctor will sell another. Do you really want to learn all about dentists? Do you want to read their magazines, join their associations, and attend their conventions? You do not have time for that. But, what you should do is publish this book. Then do the advanced book, then the business forms book and then the little books chiropractors give to their patients. You want to become known as the publisher for the chiropractic industry."

Anyone who has ever been in sales will tell us, it is far easier to sell an additional product to an existing customer than it is to find a new customer. Stay in one field and keep adding products until you own it.

Does your subject qualify under the six musts?

"I have never met an author who was sorry he or she wrote a book. They are only sorry they did not write it sooner." —Sam Horn, *Tongue Fu!*

Chapter Three

Researching Your Topic and Checking for Competition

Before you begin your writing journey, you must do some research. You want to know how much information is available on the subject and if this book has been written before. Once you see what is out there, your approach, angle, hook, direction or niche may change. This research has a stimulating effect. Your book will take shape in your mind as you find where you fit in.

Online bookstore databases such as Amazon.com list all the books that are currently available or "in print" as well as "out-of-print" books. Make a *subject* search and print out the results. Try several alternative words. For example, for a book on skydiving, try these words: skydive, skydiving, skydiver, parachute, parachuting, parachutist, and freefall. To be thorough, make a similar search for *titles* beginning with the same key words. Try several book databases.

> "Never skimp on your research. So-called writer's block is invariably the result of too little research. If you know enough, you won't have trouble filling as many pages as you want to." —Louise Purwin Zobel

After you do this, make a search on your proposed or *working title*. Make sure it has not been used recently.

Next, see how much information is available on your subject. You want to gather information on every book, magazine article, database and resource. Visit the Web sites listed in the Appendix and use the search engines such as *Webcrawler, Excite* and *Yahoo*. Check sites such as http://nt.excite.com. Type in key words and the site will collect articles for you.

> **"On the Web, a journey of a thousand leagues begins with the first keystroke."**
> **—Scott Gross,** *Positively Outrageous Service*

This detective work can be great fun. One scrap of information will lead to another as you spend hours on the Internet, *the world's largest library.*

Donna Rae discovered the Scandinavian personal-care practice of *body brushing*. A search of Web databases, such as Amazon.com, quickly revealed there has never been a book on the subject. Encouraged, she conducted more research, sat down and wrote the book, *Reveal your GLOW! Brush Your Body Beautiful*. Next, she packaged the brushes and oils described in the book. Her discovery became a business.

Libraries. For most book research, you will go to the Reference Desk at your public library. The reference section is where you will find the directories and other resources that are not loaned out. For technical subjects, you may find more useful information at a university library. Specific subjects may require a visit to a law or medical library. There are many different types of libraries.

"The greatest part of a writer's time is spent in reading, in order to write; a man will turn over half a library to make one book." —Samuel Johnson

Call the library and ask how you may access the "card file" online. Then you will have access to the listings of all the books in the library system, usually statewide, without leaving home.

When you go to the library, make sure it is a downtown library in the largest, nearest city. Do not visit a branch or small-town library. It will not have a sufficient budget to stock all the references you want.

Dan Poynter was researching a new book idea a few years back. He visited the Santa Barbara Library, quite a good one for a town of 80,000. Of the three directories he wanted, they had but one and it was three years old. He has not been back since and now does all his research online.

Always stop by the bank for a roll of coins for the photocopy machine. When you are at the library, you will discover a wealth of material. You do not have time to write down bits of information on paper. Make a photocopy and move on. One reference will lead to another; this is detective work. Bring the photocopies home and add them to your growing file.

"Writing a book is a journey. We learn as we write. Some books need never be published. We are richer for just studying the field."

Do not try to find anything in the library in 20 minutes. Each visit will require half a day or an entire evening. There is too much information and too many references to be discovered.

If you did not make an online *subject* and *title* search, see *Books In Print*. In several volumes or on CD, *BIP* lists all the books that are currently available by title, author and subject. All the publishers are listed in the last volume. Search for your subject and title as described above. Photocopy the pages. Make a similar check of *Forthcoming Books in Print*. It lists the recently announced books that have not been added to the annual *BIP* yet. Next, check *Books Out of Print*.

Review the Card File listing all the books in the library or library system. The File is usually in a computer now. Look for the books you discovered in your subject and title searches. Go and find them on the shelves. Check out those you can and skim those you cannot. Photocopy research material from the books you can't bring home.

> **"The secret of good writing is to say an old thing in a new way or to say a new thing in an old way."**
> **— Richard Harding Davis**

Don't worry when you see other books that sound like the one you propose to write. Many books are poorly titled. But, you must get all the books to check their coverage and to reference in your book.

Now research all the magazines on your subject. See the magazine directories such as the *Standard Periodical Directory* and *Ulrich's Periodical Directory*. Look at the newsletter directories such as *Hudson's Newsletter Directory* and *Newsletters in Print*. For less specific periodicals, review *the Readers Guide to Periodical Literature*.

Ask the Reference Librarian for the collection of *Publishers Weekly*. If you are researching a travel book, cookbook, directory, computer book or other common categories, look for the special editions of *PW*. Periodically, the magazine will devote entire sections to specific genres. These sections will tell you what is happening with books in this field and will list most of the books about to be published. Photocopy the whole section and bring it home.

Research the audience for your book by searching the directories of associations, magazines, stores and events. Will you be able to reach your intended customer?

Run your book idea past the librarian. These book professionals are a wealth of knowledge. Most will take an interest in your project and will suggest more references.

"We write to learn." —Bud Gardner, *Chicken Soup for the Writer's Soul*

Bookstores. Next you must visit places where books are sold. Like libraries, bookstores vary in the types of books they carry. For example, books on business are usually in downtown stores but rarely in the mall stores in the suburbs. You will also find that the larger *superstores* have a much greater selection. Visit several stores, both chain and independent, to see the variety of offerings.

Stores carry only 40,000 to 80,000 of the 1.2-million books currently in print. So the books you see on the shelves are the ones that are selling. Make a list of all the books on your subject in each store. Note their trim size, shape, type of cover (hard, soft), International Standard Book Number (ISBN) and price. Buy those you need for your research. While you are in the bookstore, also check the magazine rack.

Run your proposed book idea past the bookstore proprietor. This person usually knows what is selling and what the buying public wants.

How far back you must research your subject matter is up to you, you know your subject. For example, if you were researching parachutes, you would have to go all the way back to 1495 and Leonardo da Vinci. If you are researching computers, three months ought to do it.

Your bookshelves should have a number of books on your intended subject. Go through those books and photocopy the pages with information you want to include in your book.

Call Ingram's automated stock and sales system at 615-287-6803. Just punch in the ISBN, found on the copyright page, to check the rate of sale for the various books you have located on your subject. The automated voice will tell you how many books are stocked in each of the seven Ingram warehouses, how many copies Ingram sold last year and how many they have sold so far this year. These numbers are not total sales figures, but since Ingram handles more than half of the books in the country, the figures give you an idea of the rate of sale and are good for comparison.

Call authors and publishers of older, out-of-print books and ask how the book did. Most authors and publishers are helpful and will share this information. Since the book has run its course and is no longer available, you do not pose a threat to their business. They regard their books as members of the family and most parents like to brag about their children. If the author or publisher has time, he or she will usually open up and tell you all about the successes and challenges the book had.

"They're there, they're mine they're my children."
—Norman Mailer

A market survey may give you more encouragement to proceed. Ask people in your industry or association if such a book is needed and what you might charge for it. If they are a dealer, ask how many they might sell in a year and so on.

Before writing his first major book (590 pages, 2,000 illustrations, and 5,000 copies), Dan Poynter polled the parachute industry regarding its viability. Encouraged with the response, he borrowed $15,000 from his parents and proceeded.

Get a *Model Book*. Visit a bookstore. Check your section, then look into other shelves. Find a book you like—on any subject. Consider the binding, layout, feel, margins, type style, everything. Then buy it. Use this book for a model. Tell your typesetter (or typeset it yourself) and printer you want your manuscript to look like this book. There is no need to create a new design when you can follow an existing one.

"If you want your book to sell like a book, it has to look like a book."

You will note that each genre (classification) has its own special look. For example, books on business usually have a hard cover and a dust jacket. Books for professionals such as doctors, lawyers and accountants are hardcover without a dust jacket. Children's books are larger, four color and have 32 pages. Cookbooks are wider than they are tall so they will open and lie flat. Travel books are lightweight and easy to carry. Your book must look like the rest on the shelf.

This is no time for creativity. If your book is *different*, it will lose credibility. Potential buyers will think you are an amateur and not ready to be a real publisher.

> Milt Strong writes and publishes books on square dancing. All his books measure about 3.75 x 8.5 inches. He explains that dancers want a tall, skinny book so they can read the step instructions and then slip the book into a back pocket.

Book printers will produce an acceptable book but that book will be boring unless you provide some direction. What usually happens is that the author-publisher spends a great deal of time on the text and the manufacturing becomes an afterthought. The package design is left up to the printer. What we see today are 5.5 x 8.5 softcover books that look the same. Printers can supply foldout pages, gold foil on the cover, die cut jackets, embossed covers and many other things. All you have to do is ask. Get a model book so you can adapt an appropriate design and visualize your finished product.

Get all the specialized books on your subject. If you are writing a travel book, cookbook, life story, humor book, directory, computer book or about something in another common category, see the specialized books. These books will tell you how to write them, how to produce them and, most importantly, how to market them. Do not reinvent the wheel. It is less expensive to buy several books on your genre than it is to make one mistake. Also, to help you throughout the process, pick up a copy of *The Self-Publishing Manual* by Dan Poynter. See listings in the Appendix

"**A writer's life should be a tranquil life. Read a lot and go to the movies." —Mario Puzo**

Chapter Four

Your Book's Title and Subtitle

Choosing titles and subtitles. Selecting the title and subtitle will be the single-most important piece of copy writing you will do for your book. A great title will not sell a bad book but a poor title will hide a good book from potential customers. Both your title and subtitle must be a selling tool. They are the *hook* that help sales.

> **"If I had titled my book *How to Defuse Conflicts* or even *Avoiding Verbal Combat*, how many publishers (and later customers) would look at it? *Tongue Fu!* got me a publisher, buying readers and later lots of media attention." —Sam Horn**

Select a *working title* now so that you can improve on it as you work on your book. Start with a short, catchy and descriptive title, and add a lengthy, explanatory subtitle.

> **"Choose a title for your book at least as carefully as you would select a given name for your first-born child."**
> **—Nat Bodian**

Here are some bestsellers or classics that underwent a title change prior to publication. The original titles are in parenthesis.

- *All The President's Men* (At This Point in Time)
- *Everything You Always Wanted to Know About Sex But Were Afraid to Ask.* (The Birds and the Bees)
- *Valley of the Dolls* (They Don't Build Statues to Businessmen)
- *Pride and Prejudice* (First Impressions)
- *Roots* (Before This Anger)

Comedian Mort Saul tells this story on the importance of titles: One method of bolstering sagging sales is to republish a book with a new, more provocative title and an eye-catching cover design. To illustrate, he told of a new paperback he had seen in a drug store. On the cover was a dramatic picture of a Cossack sweeping a half-clad maiden onto his horse. In large red letters was the title: *This is my Flesh.* And underneath, in small letters, was the statement, "Formerly published under the title *Introduction to Accounting.*"

Key word. The first word of the title should be the same as the subject whenever possible to make the book easy to find. The book will be listed in Bowker's *Books In Print* by title, author and subject. If the title and subject are the same, you have doubled your exposure. Most other directories list only titles in alphabetical order.

Dan Poynter wrote the first book on the new aviation sport of hang gliding back in 1973. He called the book *Hang Gliding, the Basic Handbook of Skysurfing.* The new sport was called *hang gliding* on the West Coast and *skysurfing* on the East Coast. No one knew which name would ultimately take over. Dan covered himself by using both key words in the title and subtitle. Years later, hang gliding won out over skysurfing and pilots were mounting motors on their gliders. Dan changed the title of the tenth edition to *Hang Gliding, The Basic Handbook of Motorized Flight*.

On the other hand, if you come up with a fantastic title and it does not begin with the key word, it is possible that you may sell so many more copies of the book due to the title that the directory listings become unimportant.

What Color is Your Parachute? is a very successful book on job finding; it is not about skydiving. Golden Parachute is a common buzzword to personnel people but it means little to the general public.

"Every year hundreds of book authors begin their book title with Introduction to, thereby sentencing them to burial among their fellow introductions in card catalogs and reference books." —Nat Bodian

Most book listings do not describe the contents, so your subtitle should define what the book is about. For example, *Computer Selection Guide; Choosing the Right Hardware & Software: Business-Professional-Personal* is listed under the heading, "computers," while the rest of the title and subtitle clearly explain what the book is about.

The title for Is *There a Book Inside You?* came before the book was written. Mindy Bingham came up with the title and then she and Dan Poynter wrote a book around it. Based on just the title and cover art, the book club rights were sold to Writer's Digest. The text had not even been completed.

Review *Books In Print*, an online bookstore such as Amazon.com, a dictionary and a thesaurus when searching for a title.

If your title is not clear, potential buyers may not find your book because it has been mis-shelved; they may be too embarrassed to ask for it, or they may not recognize it as being an important subject to them.

Make your title specific, familiar and short. The title should be easy to remember and easy to say. The words should relate well to each other. Ollie North's book was titled *Under Fire*. Alan Dershowitz wrote *Chutzpah*. And Derek Humphrey penned *Final Exit*. Keep your title short and snappy. A shorter title is easier to remember.

> **"Your title should be five words or less or people have to use their brains to repeat it."**
> **—Jeff Herman, literary agent**

Books in Print uses a 92-character computer field. Make sure your title and subtitle tell the whole story and do not go over 92 characters. Some of the industry electronic ordering systems limit the title to 15 characters. Books are ordered by ISBN and the 15-character title is just a reference.

Do not start your title with a number as in "101 ways to . . .". These titles are hard to catalog and then hard to find. Librarians have to decide does the "1" go above the letters, under "one" or under "hundred"?

> **"Authors, as a rule, are poor judges of titles and often go for the cute or clever rather than the practical."**
> **—Nat Bodian**

Image. The title should project a warm, successful, positive image. Consider, for example, a book titled *We, The Lonely People*. No one wants to admit he or she is lonely; no one wants to be seen reading this book on the bus. Browsers are even reluctant to be seen picking up *The I Got Dumped Handbook*. Remember, *Hog Island* in the Caribbean wasn't drawing tourists until it was renamed *Paradise Island*. Think about image.

The title must grab attention and make a promise. Think about other products that say *Buy this hair spray and you will get a date Saturday night*. Good book titles are the best teaser copy in an ad or on the shelf. Think of good teaser copy and try it for a title.

Which title would sell more books: *Five Days* or *Five Nights?* If you change just one word, the picture is completely different.

Prevention books such as *Don't Get Burned* and *How to Avoid Bicycle Theft* are hard to sell. Try to make the title more positive. Rather than *Don't be a Victim*, how about *Fighting Back; taking charge in assault, rape and car jacking?*

The title should be specific. This is the age of specialization. Today, books and magazines are aimed at a tightly focused, highly targeted audience.

A test was made by running large ads for a book with two different titles. One was named The *Art of Courtship* and the other was called *The Art of Kissing*. *The Art of Courtship* pulled 17,500 orders while *The Art of Kissing* sold 60,500 because it was more specific. In another test, *Eating for Health* sold 36,000 copies, while *Care of Skin and Hair* sold 52,000 copies. And here are some more: *The Tallow Ball*— 15,000; *The French Prostitute's Sacrifice*—54,700. *The Art of Controversy*—very few; *How to Argue Logically*—30,000; this title includes a promise. *An Introduction to Einstein*—15,000; *Einstein's Theory of Relativity Explained*—42,000; the new title is more specific and makes a promise.

Customers buy the specific over the general. Put your number one benefit in the title and subtitle of your book and make the description specific.

Beware of working titles. Working titles are dangerous because they can become too familiar while being misleading or meaningless to potential customers.

> *Choices, a Teen Woman's Journal for Self-Awareness and Personal Planning* was a hot seller but it could not be used in schools unless there was a version for the boys. So the authors wrote a new book. Working titles ranged from *Choices II*, to *Choices Too*, and even *Son of Choices*. What sounded ridiculous in the beginning became familiar and sounded fairly good. Finally the three female authors settled on *Changes* but found that men did not like it. After discussions with a number of men, they agreed to change the name to *Challenges: A Teen Man's Journal for Self-Awareness and Personal Planning*. Most men rise to challenges but do not like changes. Consider the potential customer.

Titles cannot be copyrighted. The reason is there are too many books and too few words in the language. Check *Books in Print* and *Forthcoming Books in Print* for competing titles. Search an online bookstore such as Amazon.com.

> "Fresh titles seem in short supply as more books are published each year. A new Harper & Row novel *Continental Drift* has the same name as a 1978 Knopf novel. Novels named *Pearl* are forthcoming from both St. Martins and Knopf."
> —*The Wall Street Journal*, February 1984

Make sure your title does not *sound* like the title of an existing book. Booksellers may palm off someone else's book on the customer who asks for yours.

Do not waste your efforts competing for attention for a book with a same title. Spend your time selling your book, not competing with another book.

Use generic not proprietary names. Some titles may be part of a trademark. For example, *Checkerboard Square* belongs to Ralston Purina. Avoid trademark infringement problems by avoiding proprietary names.

A play-on-words may benefit from recognition. People remember a well-turned phrase better than a dull word group. Dottie Walters wrote a book titled *Speak & Grow Rich*. She is playing on the famous Napoleon Hill book *Think & Grow Rich*. And, of course we have seen *The Joy of* everything from cooking to safe sex.

> While drafting this book, Dan Poynter hit on "Write & Grow Rich." His search of the Amazon.com database revealed a lot of "& Grow Rich" books but none on writing. Then he called Dottie Walters, co-author of *Speak & Grow Rich*, and was pleased she was not offended but thrilled. *Imitation is the sincerest form of flattery.*

Here are some more sound-alike titles: *Dancing with Lawyers* by Nicholas Carroll. And some relationship books by Bob Mandel: *Heart Over Heals, Two Hearts Are Better Than One, Open Heart Therapy.*

What is a good title? It is one that sells the book.

Your Subtitle should be descriptive. While the title should be short, the subtitle should be longer and more illustrative

> **"The title should be short enough to be quickly readable, but long enough to identify the book's**

> subject, its level, and its coverage. Sometimes—
> particularly with books oriented towards business and
> management—the book's prime benefit should be
> part of the title as well. Most such books have
> compound titles separated by a colon, with the main
> content up front and an explanation after the colon."
> —Nat Bodian

An example of a very long and descriptive title and subtitle is *Parachuting I/E Course, A Program of Study to Prepare the Expert Parachutist for the USPA Instructor/Examiner Written Examination.* Certainly this subtitle tells precisely what the book is about.

A subtitle may be used to distinguish one title from another. There are more than a half-dozen books titled *Getting Published* but each has a unique subtitle.

Title testing. Make up a list of possible titles and subtitles and test them on your friends. Show them a title and ask them *what is the book about?* How do they react? Do they perk up? Remember that big corporations spend lots of money testing names for new products. Record reactions. But make sure they are being objective and not just agreeing with you. Test the titles on booksellers and librarians; they know the customers, books and the business.

Visit a bookstore. Look in that section where your title will be. Then look in other sections. Which titles catch your eye? Will your title stand out?

Your working title and subtitle will evolve as you write and your book unfolds. Writing your book is a great journey; you are on your way.

> "There are book titles that deserve better books, and
> there are books that deserve better titles."

Chapter Five

Your Book's Covers

Draft your covers before you write your book. To focus on who your customers are and what you plan to share with them, draft your book-cover sales copy first. Everyone judges a book by its cover. Like it or not, no one reads the book before they make a buying decision. Consumers do not read it in the store. Sales reps only carry book covers and jackets to show store buyers; wholesalers and distributors say, "just send us the cover copy." All buying decisions are made on the illustration, design and the sales copy on the outside of the book. Yes, packaging is everything.

Each year, U.S. industry spends more than $50 billion on package design. Packages prompt buyers to reach for the product·whether it is panty hose, corn flakes, hair spray or books.

Stores display tens-of-thousands of books with the spine-out. With all this congestion, it is hard to get attention.

> **"Books sell five times faster when displayed face-out."**
> **—Michael Larsen, literary agent**

The package outside sells the product inside. The

bookstore browser spends just 8 seconds on front cover and 15 seconds on back cover and this is assuming the spine was good enough to get him or her to pull it from the shelf.

Your book cover designer will lay out the package, incorporate the illustration, put it all on disk and send it to your printer but you must draft the sales copy. The book cover worksheet in this chapter will take you step-by-step through the sales-copy drafting process. Use your computer so you will be able to easily move the copy around once entered.

Spine

In the store, your book will be displayed spine-out only. There just is not enough room on the shelves for face-out stocking. Initially, all the potential buyer will see is the spine.

Today, computers allow us to stack the characters on the spine, making the title easier to read. It is no longer necessary to make the bookstore browsers tilt their heads to one side. Use a bold, block sans serif typeface. Try Arial MT Black (bold). See the spine of this book.

A vertically-stacked spine is more legible

Keep the spine simple and uncluttered. Limit the information to the necessary: the title, the last name of the author and maybe a symbol to catch the eye. Print the title on the spine but leave off the subtitle unless it is short and is needed to explain the book. If you can abbreviate the title, the fewer words will stand out even more.

Dan Poynter's *Word Processors and Information Processing, What They Are and How to Buy* has just the words *Word Processors* on the spine. These two words are enough to catch the eye of the browser.

Make the spine type as large and as bold as possible. Do not use script, thin characters or any type style that is hard to read. Consider that you are very familiar with your title and would recognize it even if it were written backwards but your potential buying public has to be able to read the title easily. Do not use reverses (white on a dark color) unless you use large block white letters on a very dark background.

Front cover

The cover should stand out. It must be easy to read and uncluttered. The title should be the focus. The cover should make you want to pick up the book to see what it is all about. The cover will display the title, subtitle, author's name and a related illustration with impact. Think of the cover as a billboard.

Place the title near the top of the cover

Title and subtitle placement. Put the title near the top of the cover. The book may be displayed on a rack with only the top one-third peeking over the book in front of it. Do not print the title on a busy background (such as in a tree) or it will be hard to see. Place the title in a clear space or strip in a plain background.

"A book has got to be appealing and jump off the shelf."
—Robert Erdmann

Use just the author's name. Do not add *by*. If there is a name on the cover, it *must* be the name of the author. Exceptions are when the author is an organization or when two or more people made significantly different contributions. For example, *Written by* and *Illustrated by* distinguish the author from the artist.

Where there are two or more authors, they may be listed alphabetically or the one best known, to potential buyers, may be listed first.

Dan Poynter writes books on how to write and publish. Mindy Bingham writes children's stories and about teenage self-development. Poynter is listed before Bingham on the cover of *Is There a Book Inside You?* This way the book can be found in directories listed with Poynter's similar-subject books rather than with Bingham's. Think sales not *ego trips*.

Hype. Some books include a line of hype but this addition will not be necessary if your title and subtitle tell the story. On smaller-format mass-market paperbacks, the hype formula consists of 12 words of hype on the front cover and 75 on the back cover. They use words such *as stunning, dazzling, moving* and *tumultuous*.

Stickers. Sometimes we encounter new information after the books are printed. For example, the book may win an award. To add value to the book, you may have gold-foil stickers printed to hand-apply to the covers. If they are installed at an angle, they won't look like part of the printing and will seem more important.

"A book's cover is absolutely the single most important thing about the physical object that is a book."
—Betsy Groban, Little, Brown and Company, inc.

Illustration. Use original art and match the art outside with the action inside. A good cover designer will read the book and try to incorporate the feeling and theme into the cover.

For an action book like hang gliding, consider an action photograph. For non-action subjects, consider original art. Use four-color art; don't be cheap here.

Use of a related background
makes the book instantly recognizable

Make your book recognizable to its intended reader. Here are some examples: The *Green Beret's Guide* has a camouflage background; *Trivia Crosswords* has a crossword puzzle design; *Advertising in the Yellow Pages* is yellow and *Easy Halloween Costumes for Children* is orange and black.

Certain types of books have specific design formulas. For example: Science Fiction will have an action illustration with a man, a monster and a helpless maiden. S-F covers look like movie posters. The cover on children's books usually displays an illustration from inside the book. Mass-market paperbacks have a lot of color and hype because they have to compete for attention with magazines on newsstands. Classics often depict a painting from a museum. Mail order books need clear graphics and type that will show up well in small black and white photographs in brochures and ads.

> **"I know when I see a really attractive jacket that the publisher is behind the book (with promotion) and, of course, I pay attention to it."**
> **—Leslie Hanscom, *Newsday***

Background color. Avoid black: It shows smudges, scratches and fingerprints.

Date. Avoid putting the date in the title or on the cover (1999 edition). When the year is half over, the books appear to be old. Selling a cover-dated book is like selling calendars: you never know how many to print. You always have too many or too few; you rarely come out even.

For now, scan in some *trial* cover art, set the type and print it out. Then cut the front cover, spine and back cover apart and insert the pieces into your binder's clear outside pockets. Your book is taking shape.

Back cover

The back cover is important sales space. Use it for your promotional message. Don't waste this prime territory. Remember that potential buyers will spend only 15 seconds here, if they have come this far. You must hook them immediately and hold them or they will put the book back on the shelf. To be successful, back covers must make promises and stress compelling benefits to the potential buyer.

"Anyone who says you can't judge a book by its cover has never met the buyer from Barnes & Noble."
— Terri Lonier, *Working Solo*

Category:

Headline:

Sales copy/description. What is the book about?:

Promises & Benefits:
   You will learn:
   •
   •
   •
   •
   •

Testimonials:
   1.
   2.
   3.

Why the author is qualified to write this book:

Closing copy:

                    (ISBN and bar code)
                    Price: $

Back-cover layout

Back-cover layout

1. **Category**. Visit a bookstore and check the shelf where your book will be displayed. Note the categories on the books and the shelves. Listing the category on the back cover of your book will insure your book will be easy to find—because the bookshop personnel will place it on the right shelf. You have the power to get your book on the shelf of your choice—if you list the category on the back cover.

2. Now you need an arresting **headline** addressed to potential buyers. You want them to relate to and identify with the book. Do not repeat the title here; do not bore the potential buyer. You have already said it on the front. Use an alternate approach. For example, *The Self-Publishing Manual's* headline is *Why Not Publish Yourself?*

3. **Sales copy**. Concisely (two to four sentences) state what the book is about. What will the reader gain by reading this book?

4. **Bulleted promises or benefits**. Promise to make readers better at what they do. Pledge health, wealth or a better life. Focus on who your audience is and what that particular group wants.

You will learn:
   (benefit)
   (benefit)
   (benefit)
   (benefit)

5. **Testimonials and endorsements**. Testimonials, forewords, endorsements and quotations or "blurbs" sell books because word-of-mouth is one of the most powerful forces in marketing. Anything *you* say about your book is

self-serving but words from *another* person are not. In fact, when readers see the quotation marks, it shifts their attitude and they become more receptive.

> Harvey Mackay printed 44 testimonials in *Swim With The Sharks;* he had endorsements from everyone from Billy Graham to Robert Redford. Did these luminaries buy the book and write unsolicited testimonials? Of course not. Mackay asked for the words of praise.

Your mission is to get the highest-placed, most influential opinion-molders talking about your book. You have more control than you think over the quotations you use and testimonials are not difficult to get if you follow a plan.

For now, dream up three different endorsements from people that you would *like* to get a quotation from. If "This book changed my battlefield strategy."—Colin Powell, would look good, try it.

The blurb should tie the endorser's background to the book. For example:

> "*The Self-Publishing Manual* is the first book I recommend to new publishers."
> —Jan Nathan, Executive Director,
> Publishers Marketing Association

Use *names* or *titles* recognizable in your field—sources that might influence potential buyers. Keep the blurbs to about three sentences. People are not likely to read more. This is just a draft; dress it up. You will secure some of these quotations later.

Forewords are approached in the same manner as other endorsements. What you get back from the writer is just longer.

Endorsements may be gathered from people who read and comment on chapters or complete books. Remember, however, the sooner endorsements can be collected the better. The easiest and best method is a two-step process.

Step 1. Send each chapter of your book out for peer review as outlined in the writing chapter.

Step 2. Approach your peer reviewers for a testimonial. Now the target is softened up. You are not surprising them by asking for a blurb for a book they haven't even seen.

Draft the (suggested) testimonial yourself. In order to get what you need and in order to control the blurb, draft each (suggested) testimonial. Send it with a letter like this:

June 10, 1998

Walters' International
Dottie Walters
Post Office Box 1120
Glendora, CA 91740-1120

<u>Testimonial</u>

Dear Dottie,

I want to make you even more famous by including your prestigious name in my new book with a testimonial on page one or the back cover.

I know you are busy and I recognize that drafting an endorsement is a creative act—requiring deep thought for most. So, I have come up with a suggested line: one that ties in your background to my project. Note that it is short with a single message. Of course, you may edit this copy, change the reference to you or even start over (you are far more creative than I.) You may even break my heart and blow your chance at immortality by round-filing this letter.

If you elect to take part, please make any changes on the enclosed and return it in the self-addressed, stamped envelope.

I am enclosing a mock-up of the covers along with a Table of Contents to give you an idea of the concept. Of course I will send you a complete manuscript if you want to see it. And, you will get a copy of the book as soon as it comes off the press. But please respond soon. I am (always) in a hurry.

With best regards,

PARA PUBLISHING

Dan Poynter
Publisher

DFP/ms

Testimonial Request Letter

Testimonial for

Write & Grow Rich
Using Speech Recognition to Dictate Your Book

What Others Are Saying About This Book:

☐ I like this one:

There are many ways to be rich: having a family, doing good, being recognized and even earning money. Writing books and speaking professionally are two of the best ways to get there.
—Dottie Walters, Co-author,
Speak & Grow Rich

☐ I can do better than that:

Signed: _____
Dottie Walters

Please return to

Para Publishing
Dan Poynter
Post Office Box 8206
Santa Barbara, CA 93118-8206

Enclosed Reply

You will need endorsements on particular points and you will need a variety. You certainly do not want all the blurbs to say the same thing, such as, *it is a great book*. List your book's attributes and then draft some testimonials to match each one. Editing is much easier than creating and most celebrities will accept the prompting quickly.

"Most testimonials are superficial, teach the reader nothing and lack credibility."
—Ron Richards, President, Venture Network

Shoot high. Solicit testimonials from the highest-placed, most influential opinion molders in your association or industry. If you get turned down, come down a notch. Use the peer review technique, have faith in your work and give them a shot. It is easier than you think. Nothing ventured, nothing gained. See the list of celebrity directories in the Appendix.

Use blurbs everywhere. Gather a bunch and use the best ones for each particular purpose. You will need three for the back cover of your book. A hot one could go on the front cover. Extra blurbs are often put on the first page of the book, in front of the title page. Many news releases start with a blurb above the headline. The purpose is to get the attention of the editor so he or she will read the rest of the news release rather than toss it out. A testimonial can be used as a teaser on an envelope of a direct mail piece. Save up your blurbs and use them where the endorser or title of the person matches the potential reader. Consult your bank of blurbs whenever you are writing promotional copy for your book.

6. Show that the **author** is the ultimate authority on the subject. Just two or three sentences will do.

7. End with a **sales closer** in bold type. Ask the browser to buy the book. Use something like "This book has enabled thousands to . . . and it will show you the way too."

8. **Price.** Bookstores like a price on the book. Never locate the price at the top of the back cover; the price is a turn-off

so place it at the end of the sales copy. If this is a hardcover book, place the price at the top corner of the front flap.

To arrive at a (tentative) price, visit a bookstore and check the shelf where your book will be. Find other books as close to your subject as possible. In other words, would the buyer of these books be a potential customer for your book? Select a price in the middle. If your book is priced higher than the others, it will be priced out of the market. If it is priced lower, it will look cheap. Later, when you get printing bids, you will have to balance the production cost with your sales price. The cover price must be at least eight times the printing bill. So, if the production cost is $2.00 each, the cover price must be at least $16.00, but make it $15.95.

9. The **Bar code** with International Standard Book Number (ISBN) comes at the end. The bar code on a book identifies the ISBN, which in turn identifies the publisher, title, author and edition (hardcover, etc.). Make room for, but do not worry about, the bar code and ISBN just now. The smaller code to the right of the big block is the price extension.

> **"The cover is your primary marketing tool."**
> **—Dawson Church**

Now your title, subtitle, back-cover headline and benefits may be swapped. Once you have them written down, you may wish to move some of them around. Perhaps one of your benefits would be a better subtitle.

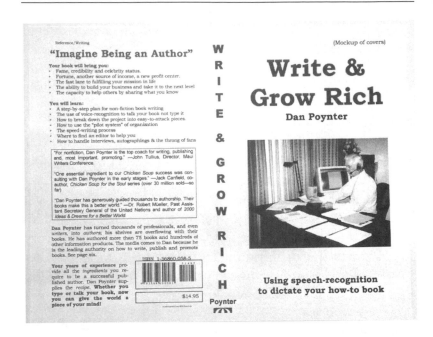

**Mock-up your cover and print it out in color
with an inkjet printer**

Cover designers. There are people who make their living designing covers. They work with color and type. They know where to place the title and bar code. They not only layout covers, they work with printers to make sure their design is carried out. Designers provide a great service and should be consulted.

> **"Always use trained professionals to produce your cover. A bad cover can cost you a hundred times the money, you think you saved, in the form of lost sales."**
> **—Dawson Church**

The mechanics. Covers today are created on a computer. Once your cover artist has the basic design, you may spend some time moving type, changing other graphic elements or altering colors. Just ask your cover artist to attach the cover image to an email message. Then view it on your monitor or print it out with a color inkjet printer. The colors will not match perfectly but you will get a good idea of what your artist has created. Your artist can also send you a more accurate color *comp* to view via a delivery service.

When the design is finalized, the disk may be sent to the printer or the design may be sent via modem over telephone lines.

Cost. Original art may cost $2,000 or more but you are buying a complete cover design not just an illustration. There are a lot of artists who will draw a picture for $300 or $400 but what you want is a complete front cover, spine and back cover (mechanical) on disk, ready to go to the color separator and printer. A good cover artist will coordinate the job so that you do not have to get in the middle relaying messages you do not understand. If this still sounds like a lot of money, you should know that most mass market (smaller) paperback covers run $3,000 to $4,000. Good cover art will cost a little more than a bad wrapper but it will make a world of difference to the sales of the book.

> **"The most common mistake made by publishers small and large is cutting corners on the cost of covers."**
> **—Robert Erdmann**

Working with your cover artist. Do not shackle your graphic artist with details. Do not say, *I want yellow with a drawing of...* Just provide general direction. Show him or her a *model* book you like and say you want your cover to be classy or rustic or one that says mystery. Then let the artist give you his or her best.

As stated above, a good cover artist will read most of the text and then try to incorporate the feeling of the book into the cover art. It is all one package; the art outside should match the message inside.

Dust jacket. Hardcover books with dust jackets have a higher perceived value and can carry a higher price. Jackets usually have a synopsis of the book on the inside front flap and a biography and picture of the author on the inside back flap. The sales copy outline should still be used for the back cover.

Most back-cover copy is weak and uninspiring. The title is repeated and then is followed by several quotations and a bar code and that's it! Haphazard copy is the sign of lazy (and maybe inexperienced) copywriter. This lack of effective competition on the shelf will give you the upper hand. Don't copy just any other books.

Years ago, we said "Write your ad before you write your book." This was to help you focus on who you were writing to and what you were going to give them. Then we realized the most important ad you will ever write is your back-cover copy. Now we say: "Write your cover copy before you write your book."

Packaging is marketing. Put your imagination into your title and your advertising money into your cover.

"Let's not help our Publishers Marketing Association members to sell crap, let's help them develop and sell excellence." – Bob Alberti, Impact Publishers

Chapter Six

Getting Organized.
Setting Up Your Binder

Set up your manuscript in a binder. Find a three-ring binder with pockets inside. Get a 2" model and add dividers corresponding to the chapters you have selected.

**A binder with clear covers
will allow you to insert the mock-ups
of your book's front and back covers**

Write your name and address in the front of the binder with a note that this is a valuable manuscript and should be returned if found. You do not want to misplace and lose your future book.

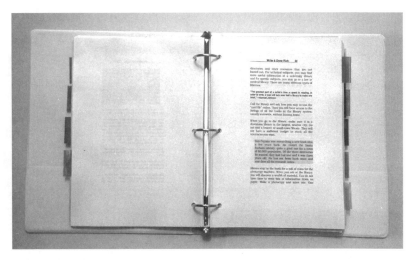

Use dividers and tabs to separate the chapters

Trim size. Try to use 5.5 x 8.5 and 8.5 x 11 as a final size for your book whenever possible. The best size for most books is 5.5 x 8.5 but you may have to go larger for workbooks and other books that must open and lay flat as well as for lengthy books. If you have just a few large charts, consider foldout pages.

<u>**Write & Grow Rich**</u>   40

directories and other resources that are not loaned out. For technical subjects, you may find more useful information at a university library and for specific subjects, you may go to a law or medical library. There are many different types of libraries.

"The greatest part of a writer's time is spent in reading, in order to write; a man will turn over half a library to make one book." —Samuel Johnson

Call the library and ask how you may access the "card file" online. Then you will have access to the listings of all the books in the library system, usually statewide, without leaving home.

When you go to the library, make sure it is a downtown library in the largest, nearest city. Do not visit a branch or small-town library. They will not have a sufficient budget to stock all the references you want.

Dan Poynter was researching a new book idea a few years back. He visited the Santa Barbara Library, quite a good one for a town of 80,000 population. Of the three directories he wanted, they had but one and it was three years old. He has not been back since and now does all his research online.

Always stop by the bank for a roll of coins for the photocopy machine. When you are at the library, you will discover a wealth of material. You do not have time to write bits of information down on paper. Make a photocopy and move one. One

Set your margins for a book sized text block

Make your manuscript look like a page out of a book. Set your margins so that the text block will be about 4.2" wide and about 7" tall.

To set your margins in Microsoft *Word* click on *File\Page Setup* and change *top* to 1.8", *bottom* to 2.3", *left* to 2.5", *right* to 1.9", and *header* to 1.3".

To make a header, with the book title and page number at the top of the page, click on *View\Header and Footer*. Type in the tentative title for your book then click on the *insert page number* icon which is in the header and footer box. Underline both your header and your page number. Then set them in *Helvetica*, bold, 12 point type.

For your text, select a nice typeface such as *Bookman* or *New Century Schoolbook*. Click on *Format\Paragraph* and set the line spacing for *Single*.

Traditionally, manuscripts had double-spaced *Courier* type. Today it makes your manuscript look dated. Another advantage of this layout is that you always know how many pages you have.

Parts of a book. Most books are divided into three main parts: preliminary pages or *front matter*, the *text* and the *back matter*. We will discuss each of them in order, so you can add a sheet for each to the binder with as much information as you have so far. It is not necessary to have all the pages mentioned or even to place them in any given order, but it is recommended that convention be followed unless you have a good, specific reason to stray. Set up these sections as best you can, so the book will begin to take shape. You will make additions and revisions to the binder later.

There are two pages to each sheet or leaf of paper. The *verso* pages are on the left-hand side and are even numbered while the *recto* pages are on the right-hand side with odd numbers.

Setting up the binder will further encourage you. Soon you will have a partial manuscript; the book will be taking shape and you will have something tangible to carry around. This will make you feel proud and give you the flexibility to write and rewrite and to improve your manuscript while away from home.

Set up your binder in the order that follows and see this book for examples of each part.

Front matter

The front matter is that material placed at the beginning of the book. It includes everything up to the beginning of Chapter One.

End papers may be plain or printed, are usually of heavier paper, and are glued to the inside front and back covers of hardbound (casebound) books. End papers dress up the book and hold it together. End papers are usually not printed but occasionally have appropriate maps.

Testimonials, endorsements and excerpts from reviews are being seen more and more on the first page of softcover books. This is important sales space.

The bastard title or half title is more often found in hardbound books than in paperbacks. It contains only the title and is a right-hand page. Until the later 1800s, books were usually sold without covers—so the buyer could have all his books bound in the same style for a matching library. The bastard title page was just a wrapper for the text. It was often removed before binding.

The frontispiece is a photograph or *plate* usually found on a left-hand page facing the title page. Before modern printing machinery, illustrations were expensive to print, and the frontispiece might be the only picture in the book. Often the frontispiece was an engraving of the author. Today this page is commonly left blank or used to list other books by the same author.

The title page is on the right-hand side and lists the full title and subtitle of the book. This page may also include the name of the author or editor, the publisher, whether this is an original or revised edition, location of the publisher and the date.

Pen names (pseudonyms). Some wannabee authors spend far too much time dreaming up a nom de plume to write under. Unless you are writing racy romance novels, you should use your own name. Someday when your book is famous you will be glad that people know who you are.

The copyright page or *title page verso* is on the reverse of the title page and is the most critical page in the book. Proofread it a dozen times! Here you will print the copyright notice, show the printing history (number of printings and revisions), list the Library of Congress Catalog number, the ISBN, the Library of Congress Cataloging-in-Publication Data (CIP), name and address of the publisher and *printed in the United States of America* (to avoid export complications).

Your CIP data block may be obtained from the Library of Congress once you have published three books. Until then, contact Jane Griswold at Quality Books for this bibliographic information: 1003 West Pines Road, Oregon,

IL 61061. Tel: 800-323-4241; Tel: 815-732-4450; Fax: 815-732-4499.

Those who know the book trade will turn to the copyright page first when picking up a book. Next to the front and back covers, the copyright page is the most important in selling a book to the trade, so make it look professional. You want to appear to be a big-time publisher, not a kitchen-based word shop.

Each time you revise the book, it is worthwhile to restrip and reshoot the copyright page in order to add, for example, *Second Printing, revised, 2001,* as this lets the potential purchaser know the book is up-to-date. Most big publishers do not make any changes to the copyright page and print a string of numbers on it instead. You will note: "10 9 8 7 6 5 4 3 2 1," which indicates to the trained eye that this is the first edition. Prior to reprinting it, the printer will opaque out the "1" on the photographic negative.

William Crook, M.D. writes: In 1994, I went back to Random House and said, *The Yeast Connection* needs revising. Much of the information is out of date. They replied, we're not interested. It's one of our best backlist sellers. I went back to them in August of 1995 and asked them to work with me to revise the book. In October 1996, they informed me that they were going to reprint *The Yeast Connection*—unchanged. They felt it was their duty as a "responsible publisher." I objected. I set a registered letter to the president of Random House. No response. They went ahead and reprinted the out-of-date book. It did not even include a warning about the danger of giving someone the common antihistamine, Seldane,™ along with fungal medication.

The dedication page. Some authors like to praise their family for supporting them during the book-writing journey. This right-hand page was used historically by writers to acknowledge their patrons: the persons or institutions that supported them financially while they wrote.

The epigraph page contains a pertinent quotation that sets the tone of the book. Using a separate page for an epigraph is sometimes a nice touch but may be a waste of space.

The table of contents should start on the right-hand side. This page will include the chapter numbers, chapter titles and beginning page numbers. You can leave the page numbers out for now. Fill them in later when the book is formatted. Remember, when buying technical, professional or how-to books, some people turn immediately to the table of contents to check the book's coverage. Use some imagination when drafting your chapter titles—make them descriptive and inviting.

A list of illustrations is in order if the book is heavily illustrated, has many important tables or if it is a picture-type book. Most books do not need this list.

The foreword is positioned on the right-hand side and is a pitch for the book by someone other than the author. Try to get an expert in your field to contribute a foreword. It is very prestigious when a person with a recognizable name or a recognizable title is connected with your book. Contact one of the peer reviewers (described in the Writing chapter) about writing your foreword. Help this person by writing it yourself to demonstrate what you are looking for. Experts are busy people, and it is always easier for them to edit than to create.

It is doubtful that many people read the foreword, but they will notice who wrote it. The fact is most readers turn directly to the action. You may wish to note "Foreword by . . ." on the cover if that big name will help sell books.

If you include a foreword, note the correct spelling; it is not "forward."

The preface is written by the author and tells why and how he or she wrote the book. It gets about as much attention from the reader as a foreword and appears on the right-hand side. If you have an important message and want to be sure the reader receives it, put it in Chapter One.

Acknowledgments are a great sales tool. List everyone who helped you prepare your manuscript and book. People love to see their name in print, and each will become a disciple spreading the word about your great contribution to literature. On this blank sheet in your binder, add names of contributors as you encounter them so none get left out.

The introduction is similar to the preface, discussed above.

The list of abbreviations is only required in some very technical books.

The repeated bastard title is next, is optional and is a waste of space in most books.

Disclaimers are showing up in more and more books today. Lawsuits are an unfortunate fact of life in the United States, and while disclaimers are not absolute protection against them, the warning can't hurt.

Paraphrase the Disclaimer in this book and do not leave the

last sentence out. Judges have ruled you must provide buyers with an alternative if they refuse to be bound by your disclaimer.

Obviously, if all the front matter pages listed above were included in your book, you would have a large number of pages already. You do not need all these pages, and it is recommended that you do away with most, except the title page, copyright page, table of contents, acknowledgments, about the author and disclaimer pages. Check over several other books for layout, especially old hardbound books that followed convention.

Text

The text of the book is the meaty part on which the front matter and back matter hang. This is the second or main section.

Start your book off with an *action chapter*. It should be similar to the introductory part of a speech. Chapter One should arouse the reader and whet his or her appetite. Too many authors want to start from the *beginning* and describe their research or put a boring history chapter first. The reader wants to know "where to" and "how to." Do not lose the reader in the first chapter.

> It has been reported that most book buyers do not get past page 18 in a new book. They buy it, bring it home, begin reading and then put it down on the bedside table. And they never get back to it. Your book has to be exciting in the initial pages to keep the reader involved and reading.

"It is the writer's fault, not reader's if the reader puts down the book." —David Halberstram

Divisions are sometimes made in long books with distinct but related sections. The division title pages contain the name and number of the section, and their reverse sides are usually blank.

Chapter titles should reveal the subject of the chapter to aid the reader in finding what he or she wants. The reader may be skimming the book in a store, pending possible purchase, or may be referring back to something he or she has read. In either case, you want the description to be as clear as possible. Chapter titles are usually repeated in headers at the top of the right-hand pages to help the reader find desired chapters.

The subhead is a secondary heading or title, usually set in less prominent type than the main heading, to divide the entries under a subject. Subheads can contribute a logical progression, aid in finding needed material and help to break up long chapters. Note the use of bolded subheads in this book.

Footnotes are not needed except in technical publications. If your book will be used as a research tool, readers may want the footnotes so they can follow up on the material. When footnotes must be used, some people recommend they be placed at the end of the chapter or in the Appendix. Placing extensive footnotes at the bottom of the page can make for some short pages and tedious reading.

The afterword is sometimes seen in manuals. Often it is a personal message from the author to the reader, wishing the best of luck or requesting suggestions for improvement.

Back matter

The back matter is reference material, such as the glossary, resources and index, placed at the back of the book. It is less expensive to revise lists toward the end when reprinting; avoid printing addresses subject to change within the text section.

The appendix contains important lists and other resources; it may be composed of several sections. As you are collecting information on your subject, add resources to this section. Add other books, reports, associations, conferences, tapes, suppliers and so on. A book with a large appendix often becomes a valuable reference. It is permissible to set this reference material in smaller type.

The glossary is an alphabetically-arranged dictionary of terms peculiar to the subject of the book. Some authors like to save space and simplify use by combining the glossary and the index.

The bibliography lists the reference materials or sources used in writing the book.

The addendum has brief, subsequent additional data. It is printed as part of the book or on a loose sheet.

Errata are errors discovered after printing. The list is printed on a separate sheet and may be pasted in or loose.

Author's notes come next and include additional information in chapter order.

Be careful in your proofreading and you should not need *addenda, errata* or *author's notes*.

Colophon is Greek for *finishing touch,* and it details the production facts by listing the type style, designer, typesetter, printer, kind of paper, etc. The colophon is not as common as it once was but is still found today in special *labor of love*-type publications.

The index aids the reader in locating specific information in the pages and is particularly important in reference works. Many librarians will not purchase books without indexes, so plan on including an index. The index is at the very end of the book to make it easy to locate.

Assembling the index is not hard if you build it with your word processing program. Simply read through your typeset manuscript and list the key words and the page numbers. List all the main headings, subheadings and words readers might look for. Double post two-word listings ("ripcord housing" and "housing, ripcord"), and cross-reference different terms. Format the page in two columns, and set the type in ragged-right alignment. Then use your computer to *AutoSort* the list.

Indexing software is available if you wish to further automate the process and there are professional indexers who can do it for you. See The American Society of Indexers http://www.asindexing.org. The index must be revised every time the book is updated if the page numbers change.

Order blank. The last page of the book should contain an order blank; place it on a left-hand page—facing out. Check this book and see how easy the order blank is to locate. Some readers will want to purchase a copy of your book for a friend, while others may want a copy for themselves after seeing your book at a friend's home or in the library. Offer your other books and tapes too. Make ordering easy for them by listing the full price including sales tax (if applicable) and shipping cost. Order blanks are easy and inexpensive—and they work.

Set up dividers and insert a page for each of the sections listed above that you wish to include. Fill in as much information as you have now. Keep adding (with a pen) to your manuscript in the binder as you progress. The collected information does not have to be neat or in order; the important thing is that now you have a place to store your material. As you add pages, as the binder fills up, you will have more work to carry as you venture away from home. When you find a few idle moments, open the binder and revise a section, bit by bit.

Now your manuscript shell is built and you are ready to fill it in. You are on your way.

> **"Whether for information, argument or entertainment, the book is considered a repository. One expects the contents of a book to be available beyond the immediate moment—for days or years or generations into the future."**
> **—Leonard Shatzkin, *In Cold Type***

Chapter Seven

Your Writing System

There are many good writing systems. The more mechanical-type approach described here is very effective for busy people. This system allows you to combine your book project with other activities so you can write while maintaining your busy schedule.

Break down the writing project into easy-to-attack chunks. Your book project may appear to be overwhelming, requiring more time and work than you can invest. So separate the project into parts. Think of these parts as 8 or 10 or 12 speeches, or articles or term papers. If you can write ten term papers, you can write a book.

Pilot system. To approach book writing more mechanically, break it into parts using the *pilot system* of organization. Gather all your research materials such as magazine articles, parts of books, charts and photos from your own files and anything you have written so far. Photocopy pieces from other publications. Cut them up and place them in piles on the floor. Create one pile for each chapter. Review the piles. Move the pieces around. Add reminders to yourself. See the Research chapter and get the needed addition information. Add to the piles.

The Pilot System

"Sometimes I turn ink into magic. Other times I just murder trees." —Randall Williams, Black Belt Press

It would be nice to employ the pilot system on an elevated surface such as a long counter but in most homes, the elevated surfaces are already covered with important things.

By now, you have lots of growing piles. Your book is taking shape, but notice that you have not had to write anything yet. As you survey the piles on the floor, you probably discover why we call this the *pilot (pile-it) system.*

Do not start writing at the beginning. The most difficult part of writing a nonfiction book is getting started and the easiest mistake is starting with chapter one. Approached from page one, writing a book appears to be a long, steep, hard climb. That makes it hard to get started.

Nonfiction books have several parts—we call them "chapters." They are related but they do not have to be in any particular order. There is not much *flow* to be concerned about. Start with the chapter that is the shortest, easiest or the most fun. You will probably draft the first chapter last—and that is OK. The first chapter usually is an introduction to the rest of the book and how can you know where you are going until you have been there? So do not begin writing from chapter one.

There are four major drafts for a nonfiction book: the rough draft, content edit, peer review and copy edit. Later, we have typesetting, proofreading and printing. Each of these drafts may have several revisions. *Is There a Book Inside You?* went through eight second-drafts.

> **"I rewrote the ending of *Farewell to Arms* 39 times before I was satisfied." —Ernest Hemingway**

The first draft is the *rough draft*.
Just get your materials and ideas down on paper (and on disk.)

> **"Writing is like making love. You have to practice to be good at it." —Morris West**

The written word is different from the spoken word. Without voice inflection, body language and pacing, we need to be clearer in our meaning. Remember, the reader can't ask for clarification. Contractions such as "she'll" are rarely used in writing except to provide emphasis. Use "she will."

> **"The beautiful part of writing is that you don't have to get it right the first time, unlike, say, a brain surgeon." —Robert Cromier**

Shorter is better. Use brief wording and paragraphs. Your reader wants the information, he or she is not reading your nonfiction book to be entertained.

"Think much, speak little, and write less."
—Italian proverb

String out one pile on your desk

To first (rough) draft each chapter, take one pile, string it out on your desk in some semblance of order and type as fast as you can. Do not be concerned about punctuation, grammar or style at this point. There is no such thing as a publishable first draft. Just get it into the computer and on to the hard disk. You will edit the text later. Since it is easier to edit than it is to create, writing is the hard part and we want to get through this more difficult creative process as fast as possible.

Look at the first couple of scraps of notes and digest them. Think about the person you are writing to. Remember the promises you made on your back cover draft. Put the information into your own words and type as fast as you can. Do not repeat any of the notes word-for-word. Some of the material is not yours so copying could be plagiarism and you would be guilty of copyright infringement.

> **"Steal from one author and its plagiarism; steal from many and its research." —Wilson Mizner, screenwriter**

Copyright covers words not ideas. If you read and blend the ideas of others and direct the collective thought toward your specific reader, that is perfectly legal.

> **"All writing should be to a specifically targeted group that you research until you know it intimately. Aim for your readers' personal hot spots, in a writing style and level they are comfortable with. Learn how the group feels, acts, what your audience likes or dislikes. Then, craft your writing in style and content specifically to your readership."**
> **—Markus Allen, The Direct Mail Guru**

Don't like typing? Keyboarding is not necessary to get your thoughts and materials onto the hard disk. See the Dictation chapter and follow this same writing plan.

Fill the binder. As you complete a few pages, section or chapter run a quick spell check and put the printout into the binder. Then go on. Do not edit the material in the binder until you have completed the entire first draft and retired all your notes and scraps of paper. As the piles come off the floor, onto the desk and go from computer to binder, you will gain a great feeling of accomplishment. It is important to see progress as you write a book.

Carry that binder with you everywhere you go. Busy people often have trouble finding the time to return to their desk and "the book." With the binder system, the book is always with you. As you go through the day and find a minute here and there, open the binder and write in your changes, notes and comments. When you get a good idea, pencil it in. Whenever you lose momentum, enter your changes into the computer and print out new pages. This has a stimulating effect.

Dan Poynter was scheduled to speak in Santa Monica the day after the big '94 Northridge, California, earthquake. Not knowing which freeways were still accessible and what the traffic might be like, he left Santa Barbara for the two-hour drive, three hours early. And he zipped right down Highway 1 through Malibu only to arrive at the hotel three hours early. Now, what to do with the time? He could not even go to the bar, he had a presentation to make. Fortunately, he was working on a new book and had brought his binder with him. He was able to sit in a quiet meeting room and get three hours of quality, uninterrupted work on his manuscript.

Ed Rigsbee called one day to thank Dan Poynter for the binder idea. It helped Ed a lot but not for the reasons stated above. Ed had been working on his manuscript at his office but was told to carry the binder at all times. So he took it home. He called to say that once his wife *saw* the binder, she became much more supportive of the project.

The idea for the book that you are reading came to Dan Poynter just three days before he left for the Annual Book Expo America in Chicago. He assembled his notes, built the binder and took it with him. The binder kept his head spinning with ideas. He arose each morning early to work on the manuscript, asked a lot of questions and sold subsidiary rights at the fair.

With the binder under your arm, the book will remain in your thoughts. Your manuscript will grow and your book will improve. The binder is an anti-procrastination crutch and it works.

With your binder in one place and your hard disk in another, you will not have to worry about the financial and emotional disaster of losing your work in a fire or other catastrophe.

The second draft is the *content edit*.

Now you have all your research notes compiled in the binder. You have quantified the project and can see where the holes are. Now is the time to do more research: Get on the Web, return to the library, call resource people and so on. It is time to fill in the blanks.

"Rewriting is the whole secret to writing." —Mario Puzo

Indicate where you want photographs and drawings in the text. Make a separate list of the photographs; you will find stock photos or take your own later.

When Dan Poynter was researching the first book on hang gliding, there was very little known about this emerging sport. Living on the East Coast at the time, he exhausted all the information sources available to him. As he drafted the text, he made a list of questions and another list of needed photographs. Then he flew to Southern California where the sport was much more advanced. Through interviews he found answers to his questions and he purchased photographs from some noted hang gliding photographers. Other photos he took himself.

Quotations. At this point you may wish to start gathering quotations. They may be sprinkled throughout your text or may be used at the bottom of the pages. Quotations are best used when they are placed to reinforce nearby text.

"I'm constantly amazed how creative a lot of people are who aren't in the creative fields. I sometimes think that we in the so-called arts think we have a lock on sensitivity and creativity. And hell, a guy comes to the house to paint a fence, and when you talk to him and watch him work, you suddenly realize that he, in his own way, is as creative and sensitive as anybody you're working with in the so-called arts." —Norman Lear

There are many good quotation books but it is even easier to find what you want online. Simply look for "quotations" with some of the search engines. By the way, the word is "quotation" not "quote," which refers to a price or the cost of a service.

The third draft is the *peer review*.

Ken Blanchard, co-author of *The One-Minute Manager* books, says "I don't write my books, my friends write them for me." He explains that he jots down some ideas and sends them off to friends for comment. They send back lots of good ideas that he puts into his manuscript. Ken is being very generous, of course, and what he is describing is "peer review."

Smart nonfiction authors take each chapter of their nearly-complete manuscript and send it off to at least four experts on that particular chapter's subject. They enclose a cover letter that goes something like this:

Dear Steve,

"You are an expert in this subject and I value your opinion. Please comment on the enclosed chapter from the book I am working on.

Please make your changes, additions and comments with a red pen. You may comment on anything, even punctuation, grammar and style but what I really need are comments on content. I want to be sure I have not left anything out and have not said anything that is wrong. Be brutal, I can take it. I would not ask for your input if I did not want it and need it.

If you will take part, I will mention your contribution in the Acknowledgments and will send you a free copy of the book as soon as it comes off the press.

I've enclosed the front matter and a mock up of the front and back cover. Since "everyone judges a book by its cover," this will give you an idea of what the book is about.

As, I am moving fast on this project, a self-addressed, stamped envelope is included for your convenience. Please get your comments back to me as soon as you can. Many thanks in advance for your help.

Sincerely,

Letter soliciting peer review

Notice that we do not offer to pay them. They are vitally interested in this particular chapter so reviewing it is a privilege not a burden.

Use Priority Mail for both the sending and receiving envelopes. They look important and are easy to mail back. If your book has ten chapters, you will send out up to 40 peer-review packets. Some experts might get two or three chapters but most will get only one. Do not overwhelm them. If you send the whole manuscript, most experts will put it on their desk with the best of intentions and never get back to it.

> **"He writes so well he makes me feel like putting my quill back in my goose." —Fred Allen**

What you get back from your peer reviewers is terribly valuable: They add two more items to your list; they delete whole paragraphs where the practice has changed; they cross out that part you thought was cute but was really embarrassingly stupid and they sometimes even correct punctuation, grammar and style.

When your book comes out, you don't have to wait for adverse readers' reactions because you know the book is bulletproof. After all, it has been reviewed and accepted by the best. And, there is another valuable reason for peer review: You have more than two-dozen opinion molders telling everyone about your book—and how they helped you with it.

One of the worst things that can happen after your book is published is for people in your association or industry to comment that they have seen your book, and although they do not agree with all of it, they guess it is OK. You want these opinion molders to be excited and tell everyone about your book—and how they helped you with it.

"There is no such thing as a publishable first draft."
—William Targ

The fourth draft is the *copy edit*.
Now the manuscript is complete and we *are* concerned with punctuation, grammar and style. Get a wordsmith, a grammarian, a picky English pro. Some of these specialists call themselves "Book Doctors." Professional book editors pride themselves with being able to take a manuscript in any condition and make it right—which may mean completely rewriting it. Look for editors in the *Yellow Pages*, *Literary Market Place*, check writing clubs and ask at photocopy shops. Look anywhere people work with words.

"I cannot think of anybody who doesn't need and editor,
even though some people claim they don't."
—Tony Morris, editor and novelist

Final fact checking. Part of your copy edit should be checking all your facts and numbers. Our technology is evolving rapidly. Our society is changing quickly. And all are accelerating ever faster; everything is changing—rapidly. More than 22 percent of our population moves each year and it seems as if area codes are changing daily. Do not just copy addresses out of other books. Call and make sure they are still correct. Change the manuscript now. It is expensive to take ink off paper after printing.

An editor can usually check some facts faster when telephoning as they are less likely to get tied up in lengthy calls like authors. To verify stories, email or fax the entire section, a page or two, so the recipient will understand the context.

"Don't write so that you can be understood, write so that you can't be misunderstood." —William H. Taft

You are finished when the manuscript is 99 percent complete as long as it is 100 percent accurate. Waiting for one more photo or one more item of information is procrastination. It is time to give birth. Hopefully, you will print 3,000 copies, sell out in three or four months, update the book and go back to press. And you will still be only 99 percent complete because our society, science and industries are evolving so rapidly.

Your book is always a work in progress

Your book is never finished. Parts of it become out-of-date the moment ink strikes the paper. Note these new-found changes in a "correction copy" and keep it on your shelf so you will be ready to include the updates when the stock runs low.

Book length. Your book should be between 128-256 pages. If it is too slim, it will not command the price you want to get. If, for example, your finished book is just 96 pages, add some resources. Do not "pad" the books but add valuable listings of other books, tapes, courses, etc. Both libraries and individual purchasers are more likely to buy books with lots of resources. Note the lengthy Appendix in this book. Other ways to lengthen the book—while making it more valuable and more interesting—is to add quotations, stories, illustrations and layout the pages with more white space.

Your book should not be so long as to be intimidating and expensive. Paper is the most costly part of a book and the price has risen dramatically in the past few years. An 800-page book will cost so much that the price will be too high and few people will buy it.

> When Dan Poynter published his encyclopedic treatise on the parachute (590 pages and 2,000 illustrations) in 1972, A friend looked it over and said: "It looks kind of big. I think I'll just wait for the movie."

The ideal length might be 144 pages because books printed on a web press are assembled in signatures of 48 pages each (so 144 is three signatures of 48 pages). Do not worry about page count now. When the manuscript is finished and about to be typeset, aim for multiples of 48 or at least multiples of 24.

Get help. Every smart author gets help. Seek peer reviewers, editors and proofreaders

> Dan Poynter used to do everything by himself. He did the writing, content editing, copy editing, typesetting, proofreading, order taking, invoicing, shipping and even the floor sweeping. For many years, he was billed as the world's largest one-person publishing company. Today, he employs professional editors, proofreaders, typesetters, cover artists and office staff—not because he is lazy but because they help him to produce a better book product.

> **"Today's public figures can no longer write their own speeches or books, and there is some evidence that they can't read them either." —Gore Vidal**

Some people want (or need) even more help, especially with the writing portion of the product. You don't think Lee Iacocca wrote those two best-selling books all by himself? Iacocca is the *author*, it is his information, but he does not have time to be a *writer*. He got help. For more information on working with collaborators, see *Is There a Book Inside You?* by Dan Poynter and Mindy Bingham. Look in the Appendix.

> **"The man of science appears to be the only man who has something to say just now—and the only man who does not know how to say it." —Sir James Barrie**

Manuscript evaluation. If you have come this far and still do not have the confidence to proceed, contact author-publisher Gordon Burgett. He will read your manuscript and make recommendations for readability and will evaluate the book for salability. Gordon is an author who knows publishing from the inside. Contact him at Tel: 805-937-8711 or email: gb@sops.com.

Typesetting can be done on your computer and you can print out the pages with a 600 (or more) dpi laser printer. Or you may send the manuscript out to a book designer, book typesetter, book producer or book packager. They all know what books look like and know how to produce them.

Once a typesetter converts your word-processing files into a page-layout program such as *PageMaker* or *QuarkXPress*, you will be able to send the manuscript to the printer on disk. Not only will the resulting type be sharper but also you can expect a slight reduction in cost.

"The best book is a collaboration between author and reader." —Barbara Tuchman

Proofreading. Get a professional editor or proofreader to proof your final typeset copy. You want to avoid rewrites now, if possible. Basically, you are only looking for typesetting and layout errors.

"If life had a second edition, how I would correct the proofs?" —John Clare (1793-1864)

To communicate corrections clearly, everyone working on the book must use standardized notations. See the table under *Proofreader's Marks* in your dictionary.

Printing. Book printers can produce your book far better and much less expensively than local job printers. Their quality is consistent since they know how to manufacture books. Their prices are lower since they buy just a few types of paper (the most expensive part of a book) by the multi-carload, have streamlined production systems and often work two or three shifts each day.

Each printer is set up differently. Some specialize in casebound (hardcover), some in perfect binding (softcover), and some in saddle stitch (staples). Some are efficient with very short runs (under 500), others with short runs (3-5,000), long runs (100,000), etc. Be aware that any item in your specifications varying from their system will drive up their costs and your quote. When they have to take a book off the line to shift it to the other side of the factory or send it out to a binder, costs go up. As a publisher, you don't have to learn printer capabilities and printing equipment. Just send out a request for quotation (RFQ), describing your book to all 42-book printers. Take the lowest bid. It does not matter where the printer is located because the bid will include delivery charges to your place. For a list of the 42 printers and instructions on drafting your RFQ, see *The Self-Publishing Manual*.

> **"If you wait for inspiration, you're not a writer but a waiter."**

Writer's block occurs when writers can't think of what to say next. Using the pilot system and binder, you will be prompted. It is like having an outline for a speech: you are never at a loss for words.

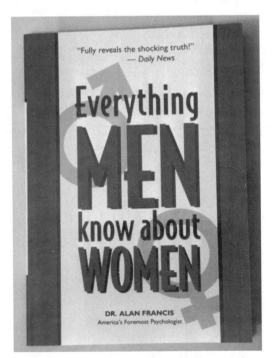

**Some books require
less writing than others**

If you just can't write, you may be encouraged by what Cindy Cashman and Alan Garner did. Their book is titled *Everything Men Know About Women*. It has inviting copy on the front and back covers but the interior pages are completely blank. So far, they have sold over 750,000 copies.

"Writing has to come first." —Sue Grafton

Finding time to write. Morning people like to write early in the day when they are most efficient and the house is quiet. Evening people, however, are more productive after dark. Many writers like to set aside a few hours for their writing each day; they set a schedule and stick to it religiously. Others prefer to write in one long stretch.

"There is always enough to do to keep me from working." —Frank Zaic

Dan Poynter likes to barrel through on a 24-hour per day schedule. The clock gives way to chapters and he completely loses track of time. He turns off the telephone, gives orders not to be disturbed and drinks diet meals and coffee. This way he does not have to take time out to eat. Every hour or so he gets up to go outside and runs around his home. This marathon of writing and diet meals produces his books in just a few days and helps him lose weight at the same time. During these marathons, he does not read the newspaper or play the television in the background. He avoids all distractions and mentally concentrates on the project.

"I prefer marathon writing 10-12 hours a day until it's finished. People who write a few hours here and there will spend too much time reviewing their work to determine where they left off." —Dianna Booher

Artwork consists of *line work* and *halftones*. Line work is a clean black-on-white drawing without any shading or screens. Line drawings may be scanned into your text. If you have illustrations drawn to order, use the same artist for them all to provide consistency.

Halftones are made from photographs by breaking them up into tiny dots. Photographic prints may be scanned in to your text for placement. Now your manuscript will look more and more like a book.

Photographs. The most successful how-to books are those that manage to integrate words and pictures into an attractive teaching tool. Unless you are writing an art-type book, you will use black and white rather than the more expensive color. Color requires four passes through the press, plus pre-press "color separations". The cost of color is hard to justify for most books.

The best photos are large (they become sharper when reduced), glossy, black and whites with a lot of contrast. Today, the computer may be used to adjust color prints so they do not get "muddy."

tilt their heads to one side. Use a bold, block sans serif typeface. Try Arial MT Black (bold). See the cover of this book.

A vertically-stacked spine is more legible

Keep the spine simple and uncluttered. Limit the information to the necessary: the title, the last name of the author and maybe a symbol to catch the eye. Print the title on the spine but leave off the sub-title unless it is short and is needed to explain the book. If you can abbreviate the title, the fewer words will stand out even more.

Scan your photos and drop them into the manuscript

Cameras. Using a digital camera will speed the process by eliminating film processing. You may snap the photo and download it into the manuscript file.

Photo release forms are advisable, particularly for pictures of minors. Permission might cost $20 to $500, but normally your subjects are just happy to be in the book. A news photo does not require a release unless it is used in an advertisement. Permission fees are normally paid to the subject by the author upon publication.

> Sometimes you will overlook getting permission, and occasionally a subject will ask about his rights. The best way to handle this is to tell him that you are about to go back to press with a revised printing and, while it will cost you to replace the photo, you can take him out. I have yet to hear of a subject who wanted to be deleted from a book.

Other photo sources. Some freelancers with a collection of photos will sell them for a few dollars each, or you can have them custom shot. Photo syndicates are in the business of selling stock photos. The chamber of commerce, private firms, trade associations and some governmental agencies have public relations departments that provide photos as part of their function. Libraries and museums sometimes have photo files. When covering an event, contact the other photographers and get their cards. They may have just what you need. Picture sources are listed in *World Photography Sources, Writer's Market* and *Literary Market Place.* Ask for them at your library. Also see http://www.photosource.com/psb

"It only hurts when I write."

Chapter Eight

If You Can Speak It,
You Just Wrote It

If you can't type, dictate. Just capture your words and get them down; they can be manipulated later. You may dictate to tape and then have your work transcribed to disk or you can use speech-recognition software to dictate directly to disk.

Dictating to tape is the traditional way and is an extra step.

Jim Comiskey sold his string of pet stores when he was 42 and soon became bored with retirement. He decided to write a book and began with a dictating machine. A local word processing service transcribed his words to disk and provided him with a hardcopy to edit. He contacted the Writers' Connection in Cupertino, California, for editing help and found an artist for the cover. *How to Start, Expand and Sell a Business* became a reality.

Dianna Booher has mastered the "Interstate Book"; she has written a couple of books while driving. For example, she dictated the first draft of the 173-page *Clean up Your Act* (Warner) driving from city to city in Florida. Typically, she plans her book with idea wheels (in sequence and subordination) and then dictates from her outline. When she returns home, an assistant transcribes the dictation.

Most people can talk faster than they can type

Dictating to your computer. Now you can bypass the keyboarding and dictate directly into your computer with speech-recognition software. Just speak into the microphone, giving punctuation and formatting commands as you go.

While speech-recognition software used to be very expensive, today it doesn't cost much more than a fancy keyboard.

"Good writing is clear thinking made visible."
—Bill Wheeler

Originally, speech-recognition software was designed for the physically challenged. Today it is for authors who do not want to be typists. In 1997, the speech-recognition publishers recognized that consumers were ready for the new technology so they lowered prices to the average-consumer level. Sales exploded.

Speech-recognition software speeds the hardest part of writing your nonfiction book—the first draft. Dictating is quick and easy if you use the organizational plan outlined in this book; you only need a plan, an outline. Now you can get the bulk of your materials onto the hard disk with your voice.

Any new writing/recording system takes some getting used to but this one won't take long to learn, and it will greatly speed your work. Some people are self-conscious and suddenly suffer from *mic-fright* when a microphone is placed in front of them.

Dan Poynter had to get used to thinking at the typewriter. In law school, he took his exams with a typewriter because, while his typing was not great, his handwriting was worse—and it deteriorated in daylong exams. When he first entered the business world, he had a secretary who liked taking shorthand to keep her skills sharp. Dan had to learn to think and talk to another person. The next place he worked they had dictating equipment. He had to learn to think and talk into a microphone. When he went into his own business, he typed his own letters and manuscripts, first on a typewriter and later on a computer. Next came speech-recognition software and it was back to the microphone again. Each system is a bit different, but skills are easily transferred and the new system can be mastered in a short time.

Earlier *discrete* voice recognition systems tried to understand each word. They required you to pause 1/10th to 2/10th of—a—second—between—each—word. *Continuous-speech-recognition* software allows you to speak without pauses; it derives its accuracy from the context of the words. For example the words "to" and "too" are used in different contexts. The software is not just interpreting the words, it is figuring out the sentences by the way the words are strung together.

> **"Improved versions are scheduled for release later this year but corporations should give these programs their immediate attention."**
> **—Chris DeVoney, *Computerworld***

Speaking in long phrases or sentences will improve recognition accuracy. Longer phrases provide more context, which helps the program recognize individual words. You do not have to speak louder or more slowly than is natural to you; speak at your normal pace. Think ahead, then speak a complete phrase or sentence and end with "period."

> **"Speak clearly as if you were reading the news on TV."**
> **—Joel Gould, Dragon Systems**

If extra words appear in your document such as "and" or "the," the program may be interpreting your pauses or breathing as words. Try moving the microphone a little farther away from your mouth.

The software companies advertise 93-98 percent recognition accuracy. Just as OCR software has improved over the years, speech recognition should too. As for speed, you may speak at more than 100 word per minute. Accuracy is higher if you speak at a consistent speed. Do not let the system slow you down. Dictate without watching the screen and let the software catch up when you pause to think.

"Writing is thinking on paper." —William Zinsser

Most of the programs have a huge vocabulary and corrections to the document may be made entirely by voice. You may navigate throughout the document, change font, font size, bold, italicize, underlined, cut, copy, paste, center, and much more—all hands free.

The book-writing process. Whether you are keyboarding, dictating onto tape or using speech recognition software, the procedure for writing your book is the same. Divide your notes and research materials into chapter piles. Then pick up one of the piles, spread it out on your desk in some semblance of order and began to "write" from these notes.

Written v. spoken text. Writing and speaking are not the same. If you are dictating your book, you must speak as though you are at the keyboard. For example, contractions are normally only used in written text to emphasize points. While you might *say* "you're" in conversation, it is usually "you are" when *written* out. And you will find the software makes fewer mistakes if you avoid contractions.

Training. First, the programs are *speaker adaptive*. You must train the software to your personal voice. You do this by reading passages from the screen for about 30 minutes. Then later as you dictate your own work, the program further learns about your voice and becomes more accurate. After dictating a section, go back and look for "speak-os" or misrecognitions. If you correct all the misrecognitions, your accuracy should improve.

Programs and publishers. The three software programs currently available are Dragon Systems' *Naturally Speaking™*, IBM's® *ViaVoice™* and Kurzweil's *VoiceXpress™ (Plus)*. For the latest details, here are the addresses:

Dragon Systems, Inc
Tel: 800 4DRAGON, 617-965-5200
info@dragonsys.com
http://www.naturalspeech.com
http://www.dragonsys.com

IBM
Tel: 800-IBM-2255, ext. SA093
talk2me@vnet.ibm.com
http://www.ibm.com/viavoice
http://www.software.ibm.com/is/voicetype/

Kurzweil
Tel: 800-380-1234; 781-203-5000
sales@kurzweil.com
http://www.lhs.com/kurzweil

Speech-recognition web sites, resources and support. Here are some great web sites on dictation software and its use. Some have links to many more sites.

Joel Gould of Dragon has an unofficial *NaturallySpeaking* site with lots of helpful information. Log on to: http://www.synapseadaptive.com/joel/default/htm

Computing Out Loud is Susan Fulton's site: http://www.outloud.com

Ruth Rose's site is at http://www.idt.net/~edrose 19/
page7.html

The Comp.Speech site maintains a lot of FAQs:
http://www.speech.su.oz.au/comp.speech/

To subscribe to the voice-users email list, log on to:
http://www.voicerecognition.com/com/voice-users/ This
site also has links to many other speech-recognition sites.

Microsoft's (unreleased) dictation software can be
downloaded from: http://www.microsoft.com/msdown
load/msdictation/01000.htm

Log on to the web sites of the publishers of the speech-
recognition programs for names of their local resellers.
Resellers can set up the equipment and train you in its care,
use and feeding.

Hardware. Check the computer requirements for each
software program. Most speech-recognition software
requires a lot of resources: much memory, a fast processor
and a lot of hard disk real estate. At a very minimum you
want a Pentium 150 MHz processor (it will run faster with
MMX), Windows 95/98 or Windows NT 4.0 and 32 Mb. of
RAM. Then run as few programs as necessary while
dictating. You will also need a CD drive to load the huge
program. Before you buy, log on to the web sites and check
the latest requirements.

The quality of your microphone and soundcard will greatly
affect the accuracy and speed of the software. You will need
a good quality 16-bit soundcard such as a SoundBlaster® 16
PNP from Creative Labs or a specified equivalent. Some
notebook computers may require additional hardware to
make their soundcards work.

Microphone. The software is very sensitive to background noise so use a top-quality microphone. Position the mic off to the corner of your mouth so that it does not pick up noise from the air exhaling from your nostrils.

You may wish to experiment with different microphones to see which system works best and is the most comfortable for you. Your soundcard probably already has speakers attached so you do not have to plug in the headset's ear jack.

Go to Radio Shack to get a 6′ (1.8m) audio cable and a female-female mini jack coupler so you won't have to go to the back of the computer to plug things in.

If you wear glasses to read and work at your computer and are in the habit of taking them off and putting them on as you move around, you may find an over-the-ear headset/boom mic is more comfortable and easier to use than the supplied headset.

Some people get wrapped up in their microphone cord. Try using a longer cord and looping it on a hook or other device above head level. Or try looping it once around your neck.

On the other hand, depending upon your style, you may prefer a stationary mic rather than a headset. A stationary mic that is not permanently positioned near your mouth may work if there is a minimum of background noise.

Dictation alternatives. In addition to talking directly to your computer in your home or office, you may find it more convenience to use a digital voice recorder when on the road. After dictating, slip the removable memory card into your laptop, and let the transcription software put your words on the screen. For example, the Olympus D1000 is designed to work with IBM® *ViaVoice.*™ For more information, call Olympus at 800-622-6372 or visit http://www.olympus.com.

Do not try to use a system like this to record a speech or public gathering. In addition to background noise, speeches are not dictated with punctuation.

Voice strain and body pain. You move your body less when speaking than when typing and you may not be used to using your voice in such a controlled manner. Maintain good posture and take breaks. Get up periodically, walk around and look at distant objects. You may find time passing very quickly as you get lost in your work and talk for long stretches at a time. Speaking also dries the throat. Hydrate with warm water.

Speak normally, breathe properly, and use your mouth rather than your vocal cords to shape your sound. Speech therapists tell us that whispering actually requires more effort than speaking normally.

"Whatever we conceive well we express clearly."
—Boileau

Chapter Nine

Your Publishing Choices

Anyone can be a publisher. A publisher might be a large company in a tall glass building located in New York or it could be you because the definition of a "publisher" is the person who puts up the money—the one who takes the risk. He or she has the book printed and then distributes it hoping to make back more money than has been invested. Your right to publish is guaranteed to you by the First Amendment to the Constitution. You do not have to get a license or register with any agency. As a practical matter, most book publishers do register by getting International Standard Book Numbers and sending books to the Library of Congress and the Copyright Office. Most publishers want to be easily located. So, whether the publisher is a big New York firm or a first-time author, the publisher is always the *investor*.

> **"To write what is worth publishing, to find honest people to publish it, and get sensible people to read it, are the three great difficulties in being an author."**
> **—Charles Caleb Colton**

The role of the publisher is to take the editorial material, reproduce it in book form, place it in bookstores and other appropriate outlets and then to promote the book to get potential customers into the stores. The publisher also inventories the books and fulfills the orders. The most challenging and time-consuming part of the process is promotion.

To publish means to prepare and issue material for public distribution or sale or to place before the public. The book doesn't have to be beautiful, it doesn't even have to sell, it needs only to be *issued*.

Your publishing choices. There are five ways to turn your manuscript into a book. You may sell your manuscript to a large (usually New York) publisher; sell it to a medium-sized usually specialized publisher; get an agent to find and negotiate with a publisher; pay a vanity press (bad choice), or publish yourself.

Conventional large publisher

Big New York publishers are good at one thing: getting books into bookstores. They have the reps and a long-established pipeline. They are reasonably good at moving fiction, autobiographies and reference books such as dictionaries. Larger publishers are not as successful with nonfiction, valuable information that people buy to save time, money or otherwise improve their lives. If you write fiction, search for a publisher that is successful with your type of fiction. If you write nonfiction, there are better alternatives to a large publisher.

Special sales departments have been established by most of the larger publishers to sell to quantity buyers outside the book trade. While bookstores take a few of this title and a few of that title, a sporting goods store might buy a carton of a single title. The interests of the personnel limit the special-sales department's ability. No one wakes up at 3 a.m. to write down a great idea on a new way to reach the audience for a skydiving book. Consequently, they are just order takers. Customers have to find them.

> **"Put two authors in a room together and invariably they will begin trading tales of horror about how their publishers handled their books." —Rebecca Jordan**

Life cycle. Consider the life you want for your book. The big publishers have three selling seasons per year. They will put your book into the market for one season—then it's history! They will publish the book and throw it into the stores for a four-month selling season. If it sells well, they will reprint. But, they will usually not allow the author to make any corrections to the text. Smaller publishers and self-publishers update their books with each printing. They will spend the time and invest the money to make important changes.

Film v. breakfast food

> **"Nine out of ten trade book fail." —Joni Evans in _Lears_**

Large publishers sell books the way Hollywood sells films. They bring them out for one season and then replace them with other products. Smaller publishers publish them once and sell them forever.

Prestige. Some authors argue there may be greater prestige being published by a New York firm. But no one cares who published your book. Have you ever heard anyone say: "I love HarperCollins books. I buy everything they publish." Potential buyers want to know if this book will solve their problem and whether the author is a credible person. They never ask who is the publisher. Ask any author whom New York has published and you get nothing but complaints.

Dan Poynter has sold books to Prentice-Hall in the U.S. and to seven publishers in other countries. He has published 11 authors and has published over 70 of his own books. Dan has such widespread experience as author, publisher and self-publisher; he is probably the most objective person in publishing.

"I see my role as helping the writer to realize his or her intention." —Faith Sale, Senior Editor, G. P. Putnam

Promotion. Publishers do not promote books. Publishers put up the money, have the book produced and use sales reps to get it into bookstores, but they rarely promote the book. The problem is that most first-time authors think the publisher will do the promotion. Once they figure out that nothing is being done, it is too late. At that point, the book is no longer new (it has a fast ticking copyright date in it).

"It does not matter whether you sell out to a large publisher or publish yourself, the author must do the promotion."

Medium-sized (specialized) publisher

Smaller publishers tend to specialize in one or two niche areas such as business books, boating books or baby books. The owners and staff are usually participants in their books' subject matter. For example, those who publish parachute books, market with a sense of mission—because they like to jump out of airplanes. If you are looking for a publisher, keep in mind that you are more likely to sell more books and be treated better by a medium-sized publisher.

Approaching and selling a smaller publisher is usually easier too. Most do not require lengthy book proposals to convince them a book is viable. They know their subject, their own line of books and what their customer wants.

Participants know where to find their reader/buyer because they frequent the same stores, join the same associations, read the same magazines and attend the same conventions. The secret to effective book distribution is to make the title available in places with a high concentration of (your) potential buyers. When a specialized publisher takes on your book, the company can plug it right in to its distribution system. For example, while some parachute books are sold in bookstores, over 90 percent are sold through parachute stores, skydiving catalogs, jump schools and through the U.S. Parachute Association for resale to their members. Usually three or four calls to major dealers can sell enough books to pay the printing bill—before the book is even printed! So big publishers are good at getting your book into bookstores, but that is of little use if your customer does not frequent bookstores.

The big publishers are consolidating, downsizing, going out of business while the small publishers are proliferating at the rate of 8,000 new publishers every year.

Agents
Agents provide three services for their 15 percent commission. They find a publisher by matching your manuscript to the publisher; they negotiate the contract;

and they may help develop the manuscript. Most agents today will require you to draft a book proposal for submission to the publishers. Proposal writing is usually a lengthy and time-consuming process. See the Appendix for a list of books on drafting book proposals.

"Agents sell hope; occasionally they sell books."

A survey of 80 top literary agents revealed they reject 98 percent of what they receive. The rejection rate for fiction is higher than for nonfiction.

It is getting tougher to be an agent. The big publishers continue to consolidate. There are only 22 large and just a handful of medium-sized publishers that will give an advance large enough to make a 15 percent commission meaningful. Divisions within the same large publishing house will not bid against each other.

"Agents are prisoners of the system."
—Michael Larsen, literary agent.

Vanity or subsidy publishers

Vanity publishers produce around 6,000 titles each year. Under a typical arrangement, the author pays much more than the printing bill, receives 40 percent of the retail price of the books sold and 80 percent of the subsidiary rights, if sold. Many vanity publishers will charge you $10,000 to $30,000 to publish your book depending upon its length. It is hard to understand why an author would pay $30,000 when he or she can have the book printed for a quarter of the price.

"Legitimate publishers don't have to look for business."
—L.M. Hasselstrom

Vanity presses almost always accept a manuscript for publication and usually do so with a glowing review letter. They don't make any promises regarding sales and usually the book sells fewer than 100 copies. The vanity publisher doesn't have to sell any books because the author has already paid him for his work. Therefore, subsidy publishers are interested in manufacturing the book only. They are not concerned with editing, promotion, sales or distribution.

The review copies a subsidy publisher sends to columnists usually go straight into the circular file. Reviewers are wary of vanity presses because they know that little attention was paid to the editing of the book. Further, they realize there will be little promotional effort and that the book will not be available to readers in the stores. Therefore, the name of the vanity publisher on the spine of the book is a kiss of death.

One major vanity press lost a large class-action suit a few years ago, but they are still advertising nationwide in the *Yellow Pages*. There is a lot of money being made from unsuspecting authors. The vanity press is not a good choice.

Self-publishing

Self-publishing isn't new. In fact, it has solid early American roots; it is almost a tradition. In the early days of the U.S., the person who owned the printing press was often the author, publisher and printer.

Many authors have elected to publish themselves after being turned down by regular publishers. However, many more have decided to go their own way from the beginning. Some have started as self-publishers and sold out and some have built their own large publishing businesses. Here are some examples:

- *Fifty Simple Things You Can Do to Save the Earth* spent seven months on the *New York Times* bestseller list and sold 4.5 million copies in its original and premium editions.

- *The Macintosh Bible* by Arthur Naiman has become the best-selling book on Apple products with over 400,000 sold.

- *What Color is Your Parachute* by Richard Nelson Bolles has gone through 22 editions, 5 million copies and 288 weeks on *The New York Times* bestseller list so far. It is now published by Ten Speed Press.

- *The Celestine Prophecy* by James Redfield. He started by selling copies out of the trunk of his Honda. He subsequently sold the rights to Warner Books for $800,000. Over 5.5 million copies have been sold.

- *The One-Minute Manager* by Ken Blanchard and Spencer Johnson sold over 20,000 copies before they sold out. Over 12-million copies have been sold since 1982 and it is in 25 languages.

- *The Encyclopedia of Associations* by Frederick Ruffner led to the establishment of Gale Research Company with 500 employees.

- *Dianetics* by L. Ron Hubbard has been in print more than 45 years. Currently, 20 million copies are in print and it has been translated into 22 languages. The book started a movement and later a church.

The main reasons to publish yourself are to make more money, get to press sooner and to keep control of your work.

To make more money. Why accept 6 percent to 10 percent in royalties when you can keep much more? Writing for other people rarely pays well. Why share the profits?

> **"Only 2 people make money on a book: the printer and the investor."**

Ask yourself, for example: Would I rather my book brought in $30,000 total or $20,000 per year for ten years? The choice is between selling out and doing it yourself—you will keep your book alive for years. You will make more money if your book lives longer than one selling season.

To get to press sooner. Most publishers work on an 18-month production cycle. Can you wait that long to get into print? Will you miss your market? The one and a half years don't even begin until *after* the contract negotiating and contract signing. Why waste valuable time shipping your manuscript around to see if there is a publisher out there who likes it? Publication could be three years away.

> **"It took my publisher two years to bring out my book . . . and I'm a much better writer now."**

The book you are reading was conceived on May 25th; requests for testimonials went out June 10th; the editor began her work on June 18th; typesetting started June 24th, and it was off the press and delivered early in August. So the writing and editing parts took one month.

Smaller publishers and self-publishers are much more flexible. Once they finish a manuscript, they take a few days to set the type and printing takes just five weeks.

> **"Do you realize what would happen if Moses were alive today? He'd go up to Mount Sinai, come back with the Ten Commandments and spend the next eight years trying to get published." —Robert Orben, humorist**

Many of the books in the bookstore have a current copyright date, yet their information is over two years old. For most subjects, this amount of time is unacceptable. You would not buy a computer magazine that was three months old. Some book buyers are catching on. Savvy buyers are finding that fresher information is coming from the smaller publishers who are more flexible and are closer to their subject matter.

> Richard Nixon self-published *Real Peace* in 1983 because he felt his message was urgent; he couldn't wait for a publisher's machinery to grind out the book. Richard Nixon had a lot more recognition and clout in the publishing industry than any of us, and yet he elected to self-publish.

If speed is important, you will get to press sooner if you publish yourself.

The third reason to publish yourself is to keep control of your book. Once you turn your manuscript over to a publisher, you lose control. Publishers sometimes decide to save money by leaving out some illustrations or paragraphs. Often they change the title and lose the theme of the book.

If control of your book is important, you will maintain it if you publish yourself.

"The major challenge in self-publishing is managing the day-to-day excitement."

Self-publishing is good business. Writing a book is a creative act; selling it is a business. Some people can do both while others are more creative than businesslike. You have to ask if you want to be a publisher. Do you have an office, the time to conduct the business and a place to store the books?

There are many more tax deductions available to the author-publisher than there are to the author. There are more write-offs for entertainment, travel and electronic toys.

Finally—you may have no other choice. There are more manuscripts than can be read. Unless you are a movie star, noted politician or have a recognizable name, it is nearly impossible to attract a publisher.

Many publishers work with their existing stable of authors and accept new authors only through agents. But it is difficult to get an agent's attention too.

**"Look, they're not interested in a talking seagull."
—what Richard Bach's agent told him after his novel
Jonathan Livingston Seagull was rejected 20 times.
The book went on to sell over three million copies in
hardback; second only to *Gone with the Wind*.**

You may avoid the frustrations of manuscript submissions and rejections by publishing yourself.

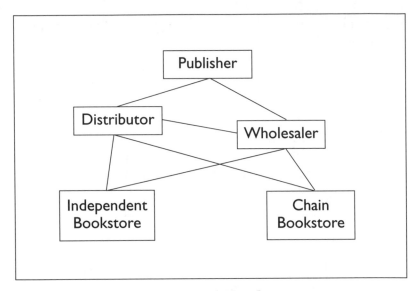

The Book Trade

But, what about bookstores? Small and medium-sized publishers use distributors to get their books into bookstores. Since distributors have sales reps, these publishers have the same access to the stores as the large publishers.

Selling out to a publisher	Publishing yourself
Must draft a proposal	No wasted time
Must find an agent	No wasted time
18 months to get off press	5 weeks
Advance against royalties	No advance
$3,000+ for initial promo	$8-12,000 for printing and promo
No royalties for 2-3 years	Money flows in 30 days
Little promotion	You can be sure book is promoted
Lose control of book	Keep control of book
Make less money	Make more money
Book is in stores for 4 mos.	Book sells forever
No revisions allowed	Always up to date
Fewer tax deductions	More *business* expenses
Good possibility of rejection	No rejection
Can concentrate on writing	
and promoting	Must run the business too

Risk Comparison

For more information on publishing, see *The Self-Publishing Manual, How to Write, Print & Sell Your Own Book* in the Appendix.

"It circulated for five years, through the halls of 15 publishers, and finally ended up with Vanguard Press, which, as you can see, is rather deep in the alphabet."
—Patrick Dennis

Chapter Ten

Finding a Publisher
Finding an Agent

How to find (the right) publisher.

We have all heard of the author who was rejected by 34 publishers before being "discovered." He or she was turned down after sending the manuscript off, unsolicited. The big publishers get over a hundred unexpected manuscripts "over the transom" every day. They have an employee who opens the packages and inserts the contents into the return envelope. These authors are being *rejected* without being *read.*

> **"The odds against an unknown writer getting a manuscript published by simply sending it directly to a publishing house are astronomical."**
> **—Edwin McDowell, publishing correspondent,**
> ***The New York Times***

Better publishers specialize in one or two niche markets. They know their subjects and do not have to send your manuscript to a reader for evaluation. They also know how to reach the potential buyer and can jump-start your sales by plugging your book into their existing distribution system, selling to specialty shops.

The secret to finding a publisher is simple yet very few writers do it: match your manuscript to the publisher.

> **"Authors do detailed research on the subject matter but seldom do any on which publishing house is appropriate for their work."**
> **—Walter W. Powell, *Getting into Print***

To find these specialized publishers, check your own bookshelf and visit a couple of larger bookstores. Look for books similar to yours. Match potential buyers: Would the buyer of this book be interested in your book?

Then go to your public library and consult *Books In Print*, a multi-volumed reference listing all the books that are currently available for sale. Look up publisher addresses in the last volume.

When you call a specialized publisher, you will often get through to the top person. He or she will not only know what you are talking about, but will also be very helpful. You will be told instantly whether your proposed book will fit into that publisher's line and serve their market.

To contact the right person at a larger publishing company, you will have to get by the *Call Prevention Department*; you unlikely to get through without a name. See the listings of appropriate acquisition editors in *Literary MarketPlace*. Check the Acknowledgments in similar books; authors often reference their editor. Or locate the authors of the other books and ask for their editors' names and telephone numbers.

> **"Few of the major trade publishers will take a chance on a manuscript from someone whose name is not known."** —Walter W. Powell, *Getting Into Print*

Call the editor (or the publisher in a smaller house), reference a similar title published and ask if he or she would like to see your manuscript. Then you will have someone to send your work to. Do not take "no" for an answer. If you are turned down, ask for a referral. These editors know other editors who specialize in their field. Call the second editor using the first as a reference.

> **"It's harder for a new writer to get an agent than a publisher."**
> —Roger Straus, president, Farrar, Straus & Giroux

How to find (the right) agent.

Many (larger) publishers prefer to have manuscripts filtered through agents. In this case, you must match your manuscript to the agents because they specialize too. Do not approach just any agent; do your homework. Find out what types of manuscript they handle.

> **"Eighty percent of the books published by major houses come through agents."**
> —Michael Larsen, literary agent

See the various agent directories such as the *Guide to Literary Agents* by Donya Dickerson, *Literary MarketPlace* and ask around. Get a list of agents from the Association of Authors' Representatives by logging on to http://www.bookwire.com/AAR/MembersA or call 212-353-3709. Locate and call authors of works similar to yours. Ask who their agent is.

"Agents would have more time to read manuscripts if they spent less time doing lunch."

At writers' conferences, try this non-threatening way of approaching agents: Do not ask an agent to read your manuscript. Place him in a more objective position. Ask "you are an agent and know most of the agents. I realize agents specialize in certain types of work. Which agents would you recommend for this manuscript?" You will be astonished at the positive response you get.

If you sell out, study the contract. The first thing to remember is that you could not possibly make the contract any worse for you. The publisher wrote the contract so it favors the publisher.

a. Are the royalties paid on the gross (cover price of the book) or the net receipts? The net is about half the gross since most books go out wholesale. Publishers used to pay royalties on the list price. Today, most pay on the net receipts.

b. A larger advance may be a greater commitment on the part of the publisher. When is it payable? Most contracts read "half on signing and half on publication."

Dan Poynter sold foreign rights to one of his books. He asked the publisher when it was scheduled to go to press. Then he changed the contract to read "half on signing and half on the specified press date." Later, the publisher found the translation too great a challenge and abandoned the project. Dan received both payments.

If the publisher does not print the book, do you have to return the advance?

c. Territories. Most publishers concentrate on bookstores and libraries in the U.S. Give your publisher any areas they cover well. Reserve for yourself those areas where they are not strong. Do not give away all your rights or you may be restricted from making sales in areas the publisher won't cover.

d. What about subsidiary rights, audio and electronic rights? For example, it is to your advantage to give the publisher the audio rights only if they have an audiotape subsidiary.

You want books for selling to your own direct customers such as back-of-the-room sales when you speak. You must get this in your contract and you must mention it early in the negotiations. You should be able to buy the books at printing cost plus 10 percent like a book club (a fair profit to the publisher for little work). The challenge is that most large publishers and agents have never heard of such a thing. They will tell you your efforts will interfere with bookstore sales. This, however, is not true.

> **"A good many young writers make the mistake of enclosing a stamped, self-addressed envelope, big enough for the manuscript to come back in. This is too much of a temptation to the editor." —Ring Lardner**

A better deal (for both you and the publisher) is to bring something valuable to the negotiating table. Estimate how many books you might be able to sell in the next 18 months. If it is 3,000 books, offer to buy that amount. Now everything changes. Publishers are impressed when authors want to invest in a project. It makes them much more comfortable about its viability. Tell them you will take 3,000 directly from the printer and will pay the printer for them. Also comfort them by saying that you will not sell into the "book trade." Since they were planning to print 5,000 for bookstores and libraries, your 3,000 offer will allow them to increase the print run to 8,000. You get your 3,000 at cost and they get a lower per-unit price. This is partnering—a true win-win situation.

Another alternative is to sell the publisher just the hardcover or just the softcover rights as opposed to assigning all rights. For example, if the publisher buys the softcover rights only, then you are free to publish the hardcover edition yourself. Run the numbers. You will have to put some $10,000 up front, but the good news is your books will cost you closer to $3 each than $15.

> **"Someday I hope to write a book where the royalties will pay for the copies I give away." —Clarence Darrow**

Another alternative is to buy your books at 50 percent off through their Special Sales Department. Of course your royalty will be less on these sales. See your contract. Normally, your contract allows you to buy at 40 percent off though the regular Sales Department.

e. Take part in the promotion. *You* must sell your book. According to a survey made by Writer's Digest magazine, 36 percent of the big publishers rarely involve the author in the book's promotion. So, get it in your contract, come up with a plan and do their work for them. Tell them how many books you want for sale, review copies, freebies for your relatives, etc. And justify the numbers. For advice on how to work with your publisher, get *The Writer's Workbook* by Judith Appelbaum and Florence Janovik.

f. Get a promotion budget in your contract. It does not matter how much it is: $500, $5,000, $50,000, just get a figure (of course, higher is better). Then get the right to spend that money recited in the contract. If you do not, some young English major in the promotion department, who does not care about your book, will blow your promotion budget on a tombstone ad in some obscure publication. The employees often do this just to get rid of you.

> "Large houses may have only four or five publicist in their department. They usually come in at entry-level and are overworked and underpaid to cover an average of 12 authors published each month. Realistically, only a couple out of the total get much attention."
> —Fred Klein, former executive editor and vice president of Bantam books

Ask yourself, if you were working in publicity, what would *you* rather promote today: Tom Clancy's new book or Dan Poynter's latest on skydiving? People are people. Accept that.

> "My experience has been that the big NY publishers do next to nothing to promote their books. I asked an editor at Berkeley what they did to market their 200 books a month and she said 'Nothing.' She added, 'Well, we list them in our catalog.'"
> —Joe *Mr. Fire* Vitale

g. Get final approval on copy editing. According to *Writer's Digest*, 60 percent of the big publishers do not give the author final approval on copy editing. In effect, they are saying, "you wrote it, we changed it and we are not even going to ask you to approve the changes."

When Dottie and Lilly Walters updated *Speak & Grow Rich* for Prentice-Hall, they added quotations from 150 of their professional-speaking friends. To shorten the book by 30

> pages so they could end up with 288 (6 signatures of 24 pages each), the publisher deleted all the quotations—without notifying the authors. Embarrassed, they had to apologize to their peers.

h. Get final approval of the title and cover design. According to Writer's Digest, 23 percent of the large publishers never give the author the right to select the title. In effect, the publisher is saying "You gave birth to it but we are going to name it." They may even change *your* name.

> Tom and Marilyn Ross were not consulted about the cover of the book they wrote for Dow Jones Irwin. The publisher even listed Tom as "Thomas Ross" on the cover.

Twenty percent of the large publishers do not consult the author on the jacket design

> There is more. The Rosses were horrified when they saw the catalog at the ABA book fair. The background color and the title were so close together, the title was unreadable.

i. Make sure the rights revert to you when the book goes out of print. You want to be able to get the film at no cost. When you have the film, you can reprint the book without resetting type.

> But it gets (worse and) better. The publisher issued the 224-page book as a hardcover and priced it at $29.95. Since it was aimed at entrepreneurs, it was doomed. When the Rosses got the rights back, they reissued the book in softcover for $15.95. It has since gone through three printing.

The contract you receive from your publisher may be in two colors and printed on fancy paper, but it is only an "offer." Only first-time authors sign and return a publisher's contract. You may make changes and return it and that is a "counter offer." The contract may go back and forth until someone "accepts it."

Dan Poynter took a distressing telephone call from an author who had just received a contract from a large New York publisher. There were a total of 21 items in the contract she didn't like or didn't understand. After dissecting some of them, he suggested she call her editor and have a discussion. Better communication was certainly required here. She called back two days later both astonished and delighted. When she asked about the first paragraph in question, the editor said "that's okay you can have it." She got what she wanted on the next paragraph in question. On one other section that concerned her, the editor said something like "well that sounds like *this* but in the book trade it really means *that* so it isn't a big issue." The result: she got 19 out of the 21 things she asked for. So contract discussions do not mean pulling the wool over the eyes of your publisher. This was a win-win negotiation.

If you decide to sell out to a publisher, read *How to Get Happily Published* by Judith Appelbaum.

These are just a few of the things to look for and evaluate in the contract. Then take it to a book attorney (not just any attorney, not a contract attorney and not a media attorney). For a list, see the Para Publishing web site: http://www.ParaPublishing.com

"Remember, all of this is negotiable. The contract looks like it is set in stone when you review it, but anything can be scratched out or inked in. If you want more books, a better discount, more help with marketing, negotiate for it. You may not get it, but you never know if you don't ask." —Joe Vitale

Afterword

As a writer and a publisher, I know that books reach more people than speeches, tapes or seminars. I am sure you have a valuable message. I believe you should give the world a piece of your mind by putting your message in a book to expand your audience.

I do not want you to end here thinking "that book was a fun read" or saying "Dan must be a real savvy guy."

I want you to resolve to get started on your book right now.

Many have followed before you and each week 15 to 20 send me copies of their finished book.

I am waiting for your book.

Dan Poynter

"The future belongs to those who believe in the beauty of their dreams." —Eleanor Roosevelt

Resources

Now you can find even more specific information on writing and publishing. If, for example, you are writing a cookbook, get all the books on how to write, produce, publish and sell cookbooks. To avoid re-inventing the wheel, learn from the experience of others.

To be successful, you must have the best tools and the best resources. We have placed the specialized writing and publishing books into groups. Explanations, where they occur, are brief since it is assumed you will collect all the how-tos in your area of interest. It is less expensive to buy these books than to make a single mistake. Most books have resource sections and ideas that will lead you to even more information.

The least-expensive place to find dictionaries, style manuals and other reference books is in used bookstores. Some of the other books listed may be out of print. Search for them through a used bookstore or an online bookstore.

How to order books. Add $4.00 for air shipping and applicable sales tax when ordering from publishers in your state. Books from larger publishers will arrive much sooner if you order through your local bookstore or an online service such as Amazon.com. Some books are available from Para Publishing and are marked in parenthesis. Order from Para Publishing, PO

Box 8206-146, Santa Barbara, CA 93118-8206, call 800-PARAPUB, 805-968-7277 or email orders@ParaPublishing.com

Ordering addresses of some publishers are given. Writer's Digest is mentioned many times. To save space, the address is given just once, here: Writer's Digest Books, 1507-P Dana Avenue, Cincinnati, OH 45207. Place credit card orders toll free by calling (800) 289-0963. Please mention Para Publishing when you call.

Writing nonfiction Books

Is There a Book Inside You? Writing Alone or with a Collaborator by Dan Poynter and Mindy Bingham. $14.95. Para Publishing. Also available in a six-cassette audio album. Also see http://www. ParaPublishing.com

How to Write & Sell Your First Nonfiction Book by Oscar Collier and Frances Leighton. $9.95. St. Martins Press.

How to Write a Book in 53 Days: The Elements of Speed Writing Necessity and Benefits Too by Don Paul. $14.95. Path Finder Publications.

Writing Your Book by Dan Poynter. This 75-minute videotape describes an easy-to-use-writing recipe. $29.95. Available from Para Publishing.

Write & Grow Rich, Using Speech Recognition To Dictate Your How-To Book by Dan Poynter. $14.95. Available from Para Publishing.

Autobiographies, Memoirs, Life Stories

How to Write and Publish Your Family Book by Genealogy Publishing Service. $9.95. Tel: (704) 524-7063.

Family Focused: A Step-by-Step Guide to Writing Your Autobiography by Janice T. Dixon, Ph.D. Mt. Olympus Publishing, PO Box 3700, Wendover, NV 89833. Tel: (801) 486-0800; Fax: (801) 486-0849; email: mtoly@wasatch.com

The Times of Our Lives, A Guide to Writing Autobiography and Memoir by Mary Jane Moffat. $8.95. John Daniel and Company, PO Box 21922, Santa Barbara, CA 93121. Tel: (805) 962-1780.

How to Write the Story of Your Life by Frank P. Thomas. Unique approach to memoir writing. Resources. $12.99. Betterway Books.

How to Write Your Autobiography by Patricia Ann Case. Unique autobiographical outline. $7.95. Woodbridge Press, PO Box 209, Santa Barbara, CA 93102. Tel: (805) 965-7039; Fax: (805) 963-0540; email: woodpress@aol.com; Web: www.woodbridgepress.com

How to Publish and Market Your Family History by Carl Boyer III. Researching, writing, systems approach, use of computers and resources. $17.50. Carl Boyer, 3rd, PO Box 333, Newhall, CA 91322.

How to Write Your Own Life Story: The Classic Guide for the Nonprofessional Writer by Lois Daniel. A guide with personal experiences told in the first person. $12.95. Chicago Review Press, 814 North Franklin, Chicago, IL 60610-3109.

Writing Articles from the Heart: How to Write and Sell Your Life Experiences by Marjorie Holmes. $16.99. Writer's Digest Books.

Turning Memories into Memoirs: A Handbook for Writing Lifestories by Denis Ledoux. $19.95. Soleil Press.

Writing the Memoir: From Truth to Art by Judith Barrington. $13.95. Eighth Mountain Press.

Your Life as Story: Writing the New Autobiography by Tristine Rainer. $24.95. Tarcher/Putnam.

Living to Tell the Tale: A Guide to Writing Memoir by Jane Taylor McDonnell. $12.95. Penguin.

Aviation Books

How to Write, Publish & Sell your own Aviation Books by Chevy Alden. Tri-Pacer Press, PO Box 840111, Pembroke Pines, FL 33084-2111.

Biographies

The Complete Guide to Writing Biographies by Ted Schwarz. Interviewing, writing, marketing and contracting. $19.95. Writer's Digest Books.

Biographers and the Art of Biography by Ulick O'Connor. $28.00. Irish American Book Company.

Children's Books

The Making of a Picture Book by Rodney Martin and John Snow. Gareth Stevens Children's Books, 1555 North River Center Drive, #201, Milwaukee, WI 53212. Tel: (414) 225-0333 or (800) 542-2595; Fax: (414) 225-0377; Web: www.gsinc.com

How to Write and Sell Children's Picture Books by Jean E. Karl. $16.95. Writers' Digest Books.

Children's Writer's Word Book by Alijandra Mogilner. $19.95. Writers Digest Books.

How to Write and Illustrate Children's Books and Get Them Published edited by Treld Pelkey Bicknell and Felicity Trotman. An anthology in color. $22.50. Writer's Digest Books.

Writing Books for Young People by James Gross Giblin. Fiction and nonfiction for the five age groups. $12.00. The Writer, 120 Boylston Street, Boston, MA 02116. Tel: (617) 423-3157 or (888) 273-8214; Fax: (617) 423-2168; email: writer@user1.channel1.com; Web: www.channel1.com/thewriter/

Writing For Children & Teenagers by Lee Wyndham and Arnold Madison. Writing formula for fiction and nonfiction. A revised classic. Marketing and resources. $12.95. Writer's Digest Books.

How to Write, Illustrate and Design Children's Books by Frieda Gates. $23.50. Library Research Associates

Children's Writers & Illustrator's Market: 850 Places to Sell your Work (Serial) edited by Alice P. Buening. $19.99. Writer's Digest Books.

Writing and Illustrating Children's Books for Publication: Two Perspectives by Berthe Amos and Eric Suben. $24.95. Writer's Digest Books.

How to Write a Children's Book and Get it Published by Barbara Seuling. $14.00. Macmillan.

Dreams and Wishes: Essays on Writing for Children by Susan Cooper. $18.00. Published by Margaret McElderry.

Computer Books

How to Write Useable User Documentation by Edmond H. Weiss. $24.95. Oryx Press, 4041 N. Central Ave., Suite #700, Phoenix, AZ 85012. Tel: (602) 265-2651; Fax: (602) 265-6250; email: info@oryxpress.com Web: www.oryxpress.com

How to Write Computer Documentation for Users by Susan Grimm. $44.95. Van Nostrand Reinhold.

Cookbooks

So You Want to Write a Cookbook! by Judy Rehmel. How to collect recipes, get organized, write, print, self-publish and sell a cookbook.

$6.95. Marathon International Publishing, PO Box 33008, Louisville, KY 40232.

Recipes into Type: A Handbook for Cookbook Writers and Editors by Joan Whitman and Dolores Simon. $27.50. HarperCollins.

The Recipe Writer's Handbook by Barbara Gibbs Ostmann and Jane L. Baker. $34.95. John Wiley & Sons.

Directories

Directory Publishing: A Practical Guide by Russell A. Perkins. $44.95. Cowles/Simba Information Inc. PO Box 4234, 11 Riverbend Road, Stamford, CT 06907. Tel: (203) 358-9900; Fax: (203) 358-5824; email: simbainfo@simbanet.com; Web: http://www.simbanet.com.

Newletter

The Cowles/Simba Report on Directory Publishing. Cowles/Simba Information Inc. (See above).

Film/Video/TV/Stage Books

Screenwriting: Fiction and Non-fiction by Gail Kearns. For a comprehensive list of books and other resources on screenwriting, see Para Publishing's FOD/WEB Document 638.

Top Secrets: Screenwriting by Jurgen Wolff and Kerry Cox. $21.95. Lone Eagle. 2337 Roscomare Rd. #9, Los Angeles, CA 90077-1815. Tel: (800) 345-6257; Fax: (310) 479-4969; email: info@lone eagle.com

How to Sell Your Screenplay by Carl Sautter. The real rules of film and television. $14.95. New Chapter Press, 381 Park Avenue South, New York, NY 10016.

Successful Scriptwriting by Jurgen Wolff and Kerry Cox. $16.99. Lone Eagle. 2337 Roscomare Rd. #9, Los Angeles, CA 90077-1815. Tel: (800) 345-6257; Fax: (310) 479-4969; email: info@loneeagle.com

On Screen Writing by Edward Dmytryk. Inside, hands-on scriptwriting. $24.95 ppd. Focal Press, 313 Washington Street, Newton, MA 02158-1630. Fax: (617) 928-2640; Web: www.bh.com/fp/

Television & Screen Writing, From Concept to Contract by Richard A. Blum. How-to, examples, markets and resources. $29.95. Focal Press 313 Washington Street, Newton, MA 02158-1630. Fax: (617) 928-2640; Web: www.bh.com/fp/

How to Pitch & Sell Your TV Script by David Silver. Writer's Digest Books.

How to Write for Television by Madeline Maggio. $12.00. Prentice Hall. Imprint of Simon & Shuster. 1 Lake Street, Upper River, NJ 07458. Tel: (201) 236-7000; Web: www.prenhall.com

Humor Books

Comedy Writing Step by Step by Gene Perret and Carol Burnett. $11.95. Samuel French Trade.

Comedy Writing Secrets by Melvin Helitzer. $16.99. Writer's Digest Books.

Funny Business: The Craft of Comedy Writing by Sol Saks. $18.95. Lone Eagle Publishing.

The Art of Comedy Writing by Arthur Asa Berger. $29.95. Transaction Publications.

How to Draw & Sell Comic Strips by Alan McKenzie. $19.95. Writer's Digest Books.

How to Draw & Sell Cartoons by Ross Thomson & Bill Hewison. $19.95. Writer's Digest Books.

Cartooning for Kids by Carol Benjamin. $14.89. HarperCollins.

Scientific/Technical/Medical Books

How to Write and Publish a Scientific Paper by Robert A. Day. $16.95. Oryx Press, 4041 N. Central Ave., Suite #700, Phoenix, AZ 85012. Tel: (602) 265-2651; Fax: (602) 265-6250; email: info@oryx press.com; Web: www.oryxpress.com

Essentials for the Scientific and Technical Writer by Hardy Hoover. $7.95. Dover Publications, 31 East Second Street, Mineola, NY 11501.

Successful Scientific Writing: A Step-By-Step Guide for Biomedical Scientists by Janice R. Matthews, John M. Bowen and Robert W. Matthews. $19.95. Cambridge University Press.

A Field Guide for Science Writers: The Official Guide of the National

Association of Science Writers edited by Deborah Blum and Mary Knudson. $25.00. Oxford University Press.

Scientific Style and Format: The CBE Manual for Authors, Editors and Publishers by Edward J. Huth. $39.95. Cambridge University Press.

Scientific English: A Guide for Scientists and Other Professionals by Robert A. Day. $19.00. Oryx Press.

Science as Writing by David Millard Locke. $35.00. Yale University Press.

How to Write and Publish Engineering Papers and Reports by Herbert B. Michaelson. $19.95. Oryx Press. 4041 N. Central Ave., Suite #700, Phoenix, AZ 85012. Tel: (602) 265-2651 Fax: (602) 265-6250; email: info@oryxpress.com; Web: www.oryxpress.com

How to Write and Present Technical Information by Charles H. Sides. $19.95. Oryx Press, 4041 N. Central Ave., Suite #700, Phoenix, AZ 85012. Tel: (602) 265-2651; Fax: (602) 265-6250; email: info@oryxpress.com; Web: www.oryxpress.com

Medical Writing: A Prescription for Clarity: A Self-Help Guide to Clearer Medical English by N.W. Goodman, Dr. Martin B. Edwards and Dr. Andy Black. $19.95. Cambridge University Press.

Health Writer's Handbook by Barbara Gastel, M.D. $29.95. Iowa State University Press.

Manuals

How to Write a Training Manual by John Davis. $55.95 Ashgate Publishing Co.

Photo Books

Sell & Re-sell Your Photos by Rohn Engh. What sells, where to sell and pricing. Resources. $14.95. Writer's Digest Books.

Photographer's Market: 2000 Places to Sell Your Photographs edited by Michael Willins. $23.99. Writer's Digest Books.

The Photographer's Guide to Marketing and Self-Promotion by Maria Piscopo. $18.95. Allworth Press. 10 East 23rd Street, New York, New York, 10010. Tel: (212) 777-8395; Fax: (212) 777-8261; email: PUB@allworth.com; Web: http://www.allworth.com.

Photography for Writers: Using Photography to Increase Your Writing Income. $18.95. Allworth Press. (See above)

Travel Books

Going Places, The Guide to Travel Guides by Greg Hayes and Joan Wright. A bibliography of 3,000 travel books. $26.95. R.R. Bowker Co., 121 Chanlon Rd., New Providence, NJ 07974. Tel: (888) 269-5372; Web: www.bowker.com

A Guide to Travel Writing & Photography by Ann & Carl Purcell. $22.95. Writer's Digest Books.

How to Make Money From Travel Writing by Curtis Casewitt. Researching, writing, traveling and selling. Resources. $20.00. Peter Smith Publishers.

How to Make a Living as a Travel Writer by Susan Farewell. $10.95. Shooting Star Press.

The Travel Writer's Handbook: How to Write and Sell Your Own Travel Experiences. $15.95. Surrey Books.

Travel Writing by L. Pat O'Neal. $18.99. Writer's Digest Books.

Writing About Travel by Morag Campbell. $13.95. A & C Black.

Writing Travel Books and Articles by Richard Cropp, Barbara Braidwood and Susan M. Boyce. $15.95. Self-Counsel Press.

Writing Travel Articles That Sell. Three audiotapes by Gordon Burgett. $39.95. Communications Unlimited, PO Box 6405-P, Santa Maria, CA 93456. Tel: (805) 937-8711; Fax; (805) 937-3035.

Regional Books

How to Make Big Profits Publishing City & Regional Books by Marilyn & Tom Ross. $14.95. Communication Creativity, 425 Cedar, PO Box 909-P, Buena Vista, CO 81211-0909. Tel: (719) 395-8659.

Religious Books

Writing for the Religious Market by Marvin E. Ceynar. $3.25 ppd. C.S.S. Publishing Co., 517 South Main Street, PO Box 4503 Lima, OH 45804. Tel: (800) 537-1030; Fax: (419) 228-9184; email: order@csspub.com; Web: www.csspub.com

Write for the Religion Market by John A. Moore. $9.95. ETC Publications, 700 E. Vereda Sur, Palm Springs, CA 92262. Tel: (760) 325-5352; Fax: (760) 325-8841.

The Complete Guide to Writing and Selling the Christian Novel by Penelope J. Stokes. $14.99. Writer's Digest Books.

Journal Writing

How to Get Published in Business/Professional Journals by Joel J. Shulman. $28.95. Jelmar Publishing Co., PO Box 488, Plainview, NY 11803. Tel: (516) 822-6861.

Magazine Writing

Freelance Writing for Magazines and Newspapers by Marcia Yudkin. A plan for selling your work. Resources. $11.00. HarperCollins Publishers.

Magazine Writing That Sells by Don McKinney. $16.95. Writer's Digest Books.

Complete Guide to Magazine Article Writing by John M. Wilson. $17.99. Writer's Digest Books.

Beginner's Guide to Writing & Selling Quality Features by Charlotte Digregorio. A simple course in freelancing for newspapers and magazines. $12.95. Civetta Press, PO Box 1043-P, Portland, OR 97207-1043. Tel: (503) 228-6649.

Newsletter & Newpaper Writing and Publishing

Publishing Newsletters by Howard Penn Hudson. 224 pages. $39.95. H&M Publishing, 44 West Market Street, PO Box 311, Rhinebeck, N.Y. 12572 Tel: (800) 572-3451; Fax: (914) 876-2561; email: HPHudson@aol.com

The Newsletter Handbook; How to Produce a Successful Newsletter by Wesley Dorsheimer. 194 pages, $14.95. Hippocrene Books. Tel: (201) 568-5194; Tel: (201) 894-5406.

Newsletter Sourcebook by Mark Beach. 137 pages. $29.95. Writer's Digest Books.

Editing Your Newsletter by Mark Beech. $22.95. Writer's Digest Books.

Success in Newsletter Publishing; A Practical Guide by Frederick D. Goss. $39.50. Newsletter. Association, 1401 Wilson Blvd., #403, Arlington, VA 22209. Tel: (800) 356-9302.

How to Do Leaflets, Newletters & Newspapers by Nancy Brigham. $14.95. Writer's Digest Books.

Also contact *Newsletter on Newsletters*, Howard Penn Hudson, PO Box 311, Rhinebeck, NY 12572. Tel: (800) 572-3451 or (914) 876-2081.

Calendar Publishing

Publishing & Marketing Your Calendar: How to Produce and Sell a Profitable Calendar by Calendar Marketing Association. $69.95. 710 Ogden, Suite #600, Naperville, IL 60563. Tel: (630) 369-2406 or (800) 828-8225; Email: cma@b-online.com; Web: www.calendar marketplace.com

Greeting Cards

How to Write & Sell Greeting Cards, Bumper Stickers, T-Shirts & Other Fun Stuff by Molly Wigand. $15.99. Writer's Digest Books.

The Complete Guide to Greeting Card Design & Illustration by Eva Szela. $29.99. Writer's Digest Books.

Writing Comedy Greeting Cards That Sell. Two audiotapes by Gordon Burgett. $34.95. Communications Unlimited, PO Box 6405-P, Santa Maria, CA 93456. Tel: (805) 937-8711; Fax; (805) 937-3035.

Contracting/Legal

Business Guide to Copyright Law by Woody Young. Complete explanations with forms. $14.95. Joy Publishing (Para Publishing).

The Copyright Permission and Libel Handbook by Lloyd J. Jassin and Steven C. Schechter. $14.95. John Wiley & Sons.

Business and Legal Forms for Authors & Self-Publishers by Tad Crawford. Has actual tear-out forms and contracts. $19.95. Allworth Press. (Para Publishing)

Business and Legal Forms for Graphic Designers by Tad Crawford. $22.95. Writer's Digest Books.

Publishing Agreements by Charles Clark. Sample contracts with explanations. International. $29.95. New Amsterdam Books. (Para Publishing)

Publishing Contracts on Disk by Dan Poynter. Twenty-two contracts for $29.95. Now you do not even have to type these lengthy documents. (ParaPublishing)

Selling Information

Writer's Market: 4000 Places to Sell What You Write edited by Kristen Holm. $27.99. Writer's Digest Books.

How to Make a Whole Lot More than $1,000,000 Writing,

Commissioning, Publishing and Selling 'How-To' Information by Jeffrey Lant. $39.95. (Para Publishing)

A Beginner's Guide to Getting Published by Kirk Polking. $11.95. Writer's Digest Books.

The Writer's Handbook. How and where to sell magazine articles, poetry, greeting card verses, fillers, scripts and book manuscripts. An anthology of helpful chapters with a lengthy directory of resources. $30.70 ppd. The Writer, 120 Boylston Street, Boston, MA 02116. Tel: (617) 423-3157 or (888) 273-8214; Fax: (617) 423-2168; email: writer@user1.channel1.com; Web: www.channel1.com /thewriter/

Money for Writer$ edited by Billot. Includes grants, awards, prizes, contests, scholarships, retreats, conferences and Internet information. $19.95. Henry Holt.

The Writer's Resource Handbook by Daniel Grant. Includes career assistance, grants and awards, writers-in-residence programs, creative writing programs, legal and accounting services and insurance. $19.95. Allworth Press.

Getting Published, The Acquisition Process at University Presses by Paul Parsons. $33.00. The University of Tennessee Press, 293 Communications Building, Knoxville, TN 37996-0325. Fax: (423) 974-3724; email: jsiler@utk.edu; Web: www.lib.utk.edu/utk gophers/utpress

Book Publishing

The Self-Publishing Manual, How to Write, Print & Sell Your Own Book by Dan Poynter. The complete manual on book production, marketing and distributing. Tenth revised edition, 464 pages. $19.95. (Para Publishing) Call 800-PARAPUB. See http://www.Para Publishing.com

Financial Feasibility in Book Publishing by Robert Follett presents a step-by-step method for evaluating the financial future of new book projects. Worksheets, guidelines, projection methods, rules of thumb and estimating methods with explanations to help you decide whether your book will make money. 39 pages $14.95 (Para Publishing)

Self-Publishing to Niche Markets by Gordon Burgett. $14.95. Communications Unlimited. (Para Publishing)

How to Get Happily Published by Judith Appelbaum. How to write, find a publisher or locate an agent. $11.95. Harper & Row. (Para Publishing)

Mastering the Business of Writing: A Leading Literary Agent Reveals the Secrets of Success by Richard Curtis. $18.95. Allworth Press. 10 East 23rd Street, New York, New York, 10010. Tel: (212) 777-8395; Fax: (212) 777-8261; email: PUB@allworth.com; Web: http://www.all worth.com.

The Shortest Distance Between You and a Published Book: 20 Steps to Success by Susan Page. $13.00. Broadway Books.

The Portable Writers' Conference: Your Guide to Getting and Staying Published edited by Stephen Blake Mettee. Great advice from over 45 editors, agents and authors. $19.95. Quill Driver Books/Word Dancer Press, Inc., 950 N. Van Ness, PO Box 4638, Fresno, CA 93744. Tel: (800) 497-4909.

The Young Author's Do-it-Yourself Book: How to write, illustrate & produce your own book by Donna Guthrie, et. al. $15.40 Millbrook Press, 2 Old New Milford Road, Brookfield, CT 06804. Web: www.neca.com/mall/millbrook

Book Proposals

How to Write a Book Proposal by Michael Larsen. Examples and resources to help you approach a publisher or agent. $14.99 Writer's Digest Books.

Nonfiction Book Proposals Anybody Can Write: How to Get a Contract & Advance Before You Write Your Book by Elizabeth Lyon. $14.95. Blue Heron Publishing, 24450 NW Hansen Rd, Hillsboro, OR 97124.

Books on Speech Recognition

Order from the publisher, visit a local bookstore or log on to an online bookstore.

The Essential SimplySpeaking Gold by Susan Fulton, ISBN 1-888725-08-7, 8.5 x 8, 124-pages. How to use IBM's popular speech recognition package for dictation rather than keyboarding. Dozens of screen shots and illustrations. $18.95

Begin Dictation Using ViaVoice Gold – Susan Fulton, ISBN 1-888725-10-9, 8.5 x 8, 230-pages, using IBM's popular *continuous speech* recognition package for dictation rather than keyboarding. Over a hundred screen shots and illustrations. $28.95

These Susan Fulton books are published by Science & Humanities Press, Dr. Bud Banis, Tel: 314-394-4950; email: banis@banis-associates.com

The Computer Speech Book by Esther Schindler. 312-pages with disk. 1996. $39.95

Speech Recognition: The Future Now! by Michael Koerner. 306-pages. 1997. $49.95.

Write & Grow Rich, Using Speech-Recognition To Dictate Your How-To Book by Dan Poynter. Para Publishing Tel: 800-PARAPUB; orders@ParaPublishing.com

Audiotapes On Writing

Audiotapes from A Cappela Publishing, PO Box 3691, Sarasota, FL 34234; Tel/Fax: (941) 361-3481; email: acappub@aol.com; Web: http://www.acappela.com

Why Your Book Doesn't Work (1 hour)

Openings that Hook Readers (1 hour)

Choosing Your Voice (1 hour)

Bringing Your Characters to Life (1 hour)

Plots That Intrigue (1 hour)

Writing Your Own Life Story (4 hours; not sold separately)

Prices: Single tape—$15.00; any two tapes—$27.00; any four tapes—$45.00

Bird by Bird: Some Instructions on Writing and Life by Anne Lamott. Step-by-step pointers on how to live a writer's life. An inspirational guide. Two cassettes. $17.95. Audio Partners Publishing.

Audio tapes from Para Publishing

Book Writing and Publishing (audio tape). Dan Poynter on how to write and publish books. Reasons to write a book, what to write, how to write, publishing options, how to self-publish and the secrets of successful self-publishing. One 76-minute cassette with resources. ISBN 0-915516-75-6 (Tape P-101). $9.95

Your Book Publishing Choices (audio tape). Dan Poynter discusses your choices: sending your manuscript to a large (New York) publisher, a medium sized specialized publisher, a vanity publisher, an agent, or self-publishing—doing it yourself. He tells the four things you must do if you sell out to a big publisher and shares the seven secrets to successful self-publishing. One 60-minute cassette with resources. ISBN 0-915516-76-4 (Tape P-103) $9.95

Is There a Book Inside You? (audio tapes & book) by Dan Poynter and Mindy Bingham is a step-by-step plan for writing your book alone or with a collaborator. ISBN 0-915516-73-X (Tape P-102 and book) $69.95

Building & Running a Tight Ship. Dan Poynter describes his eleven-point plan for successfully operating your publishing company. Resources. ISBN 0-915516-82-9 (Tape P-104) $9.95

Non-Traditional Book Markets (audio tape). Dan Poynter changes your thinking about marketing books as he has you looking beyond the bookstores. ISBN 1-56860-002-X (Tape P-105) $9.95

The Future of Publishing (audio tape). Dan Poynter describes what is happening and shows you how to profit from the changes. ISBN 1-56860-007-0 (Tape P-106) $9.95

Books, tapes, etc. listed with Para Publishing in parenthesis are available from Para Publishing, PO Box 8206-146, Santa Barbara, CA 93118-8206 USA; Tel: (805) 968-7277; Fax: (805) 968-1379; orders@ ParaPublishing.com

Brochures on books of interest to writers and publishers are available from:

Para Publishing, PO Box 8206-146, Santa Barbara, CA 93118-8206. Tel: 800-PARAPUB. Info@ParaPublishing.com; http://www.Para Publishing.com

R.R. Bowker Co., 121 Chanlon Rd., New Providence, NJ 07974. Tel: (888) 269-5372; Web: www.bowker.com

Dustbooks, PO Box 100 Paradise, CA 95967. Tel: (800) 477-6110; Fax: (530) 877-0222; email: dustbooks@telis.org; Web: www.dust books.com

Gale Research Co., Book Tower, Detroit, MI 48226.

The Writer, 120 Boylston Street, Boston, MA 02116. Tel: (617) 423-3157 or (888) 273-8214; Fax: (617) 423-2168; email: writer@user1. channel1.com; Web: www.channel1.com/thewriter/

Writer's Digest Books, 1507 Dana Avenue, Cincinnati, OH 45207.

Reference books and directories may be used and previewed at the Reference Desk in your local public library. Write the publishers for ordering details.

From R.R. Bowker Co., 121 Chanlon Rd., New Providence, NJ 07974. Tel: (888) 269-5372 Web: www.bowker.com

Literary MarketPlace. Very important. Lists agents, artists, associations, book clubs, reviewers, exporters, magazines, newspapers, news services, radio and TV, and many other services. Annual.

International Literary Market Place. Lists publishers, agents, suppliers, etc. in 160 countries outside the U.S. and Canada.

Books in Print. Lists all the books currently available by subject, title and author. Annual

Subject Guide to Forthcoming Books. A quarterly preview of *Books in Print.*

From Dustbooks, PO Box 100 Paradise, CA 95967. Tel: (800) 477-6110; Fax: (530) 877-0222; email: dustbooks@telis.org; Web: www.dust books.com

International Directory of Little Magazines and Small Presses

Small Press Record of Books in Print

Directory of Small Press/Magazine Editors & Publishers

Directory of Poetry Publishers

Magazines and newsletters for authors. Write for a sample copy and current subscription rates.

Small Press Review, PO Box 100 Paradise, CA 95967. Tel: (800) 477-6110; Fax: (530) 877-0222; email: dustbooks@telis.org; Web: www.dustbooks.com

Writer's Digest, 1507 Dana Avenue, Cincinnati, OH 45207.

The Writer, 120 Boylston Street, Boston, MA 02116. Tel: (617) 423-3157 or (888) 273-8214; Fax: (617) 423-2168 email: writer@user1. channel1.com; Web: www.channel1.com/thewriter/

Writer's Journal, PO Box 25376, Saint Paul, MN 55125. Tel: (612) 730-4280.

Pamphlets and reports of interest to authors. Write for latest prices.

P.E.N. American Center, 568 Broadway, Suite #401, New York, NY 10012. Tel: (212) 334-1660; Fax: (212) 334-2181; email: pen@echony. com; Web: www.pen.org

National Endowment for the Arts, Literature Program, 2401 E Street NW, Washington, DC 20506. Assistance, fellowships and residences for writers.

Poets & Writers, 72 Spring Street, New York, NY 10012. Tel: (212) 226-3586 or (800) 666-2268; Fax: (212) 226-3963; email: infocenter@pwonline.com or pwsubs@aol.com; Web: www.pw.org
Grants and Awards Available to American Writers
A Writer's Guide to Copyright
Writers Conferences: An Annual Guide to Literary Conferences.
Writer's Digest Books, 1507 Dana Avenue, Cincinnati, OH 45207.
Getting Started in Writing
Jobs & Opportunities for Writers
Should You Pay to Have it Published?

Writers Conferences. Maui Writers' Conference (Labor Day weekend), PO Box 1118, Kihea, HI 96753. Tel: (808) 879-0061; Fax: (808) 879-6233; email: writers@maui.net; Web: http://www.maui writers.com

Santa Barbara Writers' Conference (third week of June), PO Box 304, Carpinteria, CA 93014. Tel: (805) 684-2250.

The William Saroyan Writers Conference (late March), Writer's International Network, PO Box 5331, Fresno, CA 93755. Tel: (209) 224-2516. Presented in Association with *Publishers Weekly*.

Each year, *Writer's Digest* publishes a complete guide to Writers' Conferences, Seminars and Workshops. Write or call for more information. *Writer's Digest*, 1507 Dana Avenue, Cincinnati, OH 45207. Tel: (513) 531-2222; email: writersdigest@fwpubs.com

Professional organizations. Write for an application and inquire about benefits and dues. Many associations publish a magazine or newsletter. For a more complete list, see *Writer's Market*.

Mystery Writers of America, 17 E. 47th Street, 6th Floor, New York, NY 10017. Tel: (212) 888-8171; Fax: (212) 888-8107; Web: www.mysterywriters.org/

Sisters in Crime, PO Box 442124, Lawrence, KS 66044. Tel: (913) 842-1325.

Western Writers of America, 256 Braeburst Circle, Marble Falls, TX 78654. Tel: (615) 791-1444; Web: http://www.imt.net/~gedison/wwa/html

Media Research Center: http://www.mediaresearch.org

Midwest Review of Books & Jim Cox: http://www.execpc.com/ ~mbr/bookwatch/

My Virtual Reference Desk: http://www.refdesk.com/facts.html

Para Publishing & Dan Poynter: http://www.ParaPublishing.com/ welcome/publisher/WGR

The Small Publishers, Artists and Writers Network (SPAWN): http://www.spawn.org

Writers Guild of America: http://www.wga.org/

Writer's Resources: http://www.interlog.com/books.html

Online Bookstores

Amazon.com: http://www.Amazon.com

Barnes & Noble: http://www.BarnesAndNoble.com

Borders: http://www.Borders.com

Celebrity *Address* **Directories** for getting testimonials. Here are the directories we have been able to locate. Contact their publishers and look for them at the Reference Desk of your public library.

Celebrity Directory. Over 8,000 names and addresses. Axiom Information Resources, Terry Robinson, PO Box 8015, Ann Arbor, MI 48107. Tel: (313) 761-4842.

VIP Address Book by James Wiggins. Over 20,000 names and addresses. Associated Media Companies, PO Box 489, Gleneden Beach, OR 97388. Tel: (541) 764-4233.

The Address Book #8, How to Reach Anyone Who Is Anyone by Michael Levine. Over 3,500 names and addresses. Berkeley Publications. Tel: (800) 631-8571.

The Ultimate Black Book by Godfrey Harris. Lists organizations through which you can find many numbers. The Americas Group, 9200 Sunset Blvd., #404, Los Angeles, CA 90069. Tel: (800) 966-7716 or (310) 278-8038. ISBN: 0-935047-05-0

Bob Barry's Celebrity Almanac, 7th edition, $15.95 + $3.50 postage. Over 10,000 entries. B&B Publishing, PO Box 96, Walworth, WI 53184. Tel: (800) FUN FACT. ISBN: 1-880190-51-6.

Celebrity Bulletin, Celebrity Service Int'l, 250 West 57th Street, Suite 819, New York, New York 10107. Tel: (212) 757-7979; Fax: (212) 956-5980

http://www.celebrity-addresses.com lists the home, email, etc. addresses (where known) of more than 12,000 celebrities. Also see http://www.four11.com

To reach the agent of a film or TV actor, call the Screen Actors Guild at (213) 954-1600.

Index

Abbreviations, list of: 81
Acknowledgments: 81, 132
Addendum: 84
Advance: 134
Afterword: 83, 141
Agent: 121, Chapter 10
Appendix: 84
Artwork: 104
Author's name: 58, 68
Author's notes: 84
Autographing: 20

Back cover: 60
Back matter: 84
Barcode: 69
Bastard title: 77, 81
Benefits: 20, 63
Bibliography: 84
Binder: Chapter 6, 91, 92
Blurbs: 68
Book length: 98
Book, parts of: 74
Bookstore: 32, 41, 128

Cameras: 105
Category, book: 63
Chapter titles: 83
Choices, publishing: Chapter 9
CIP data block: 78
Colophon: 85
Color: 60

Computer: 113
Content edit: 93
Contract: 134
Control: 126
Copy edit: 97
Copyright: 50, 91, 117
Cost to print: 13
Cover: Chapter 5, 70, 138
Cover outline: 53
Cover, cost: 71
Cover, date on: 60
Credibility: 12

Designers, cover: 70, 71
Dictating: Chapter 8, 91, 108
Disclaimers: 81
Distributors: 128
Divisions: 83
Doctors, book: 97
Drafts: 89
Dragon: 112
Dust jacket: 72

End papers: 77
Endorsements: 63, 65
Errata: 84
Expertise: 29

Fact checking: 97
Fame: 11
Fiction: 27

Field, one: 33
Finding time: 103
Focusing: 30
Footnotes: 83
Foreword: 64, 80
Fortune: 13
Front cover: 56
Frontispiece: 78
Front matter: 77

Glossary: 84

Halftones: 104
Hardcover: 14
Hardware: 113
Hazards of being published: 20
Headline: 63
Help: 99
Helping others: 15
How much: 13
Hype: 58

IBM: 112
Illustrations: 59, 80
Index: 85
Information provider: 33
Ingram: 42
Interviews: 19
Introduction: 81

Journey of book: 25

Key word: 46
Keyboarding: 91
Kurzweil: 112

Large publisher: 118
Layout, page: 75, 76
Library: 38
Life cycle: 119
Line drawings: 104

Manuscript evaluation: 100
Manuscript is complete: 105, 107
Margins: 75
Market size: 32
Market survey: 43
Medium-sized publisher: 120
Microphone: 114
Model book: 41

NaturallySpeaking: 112
Nonfiction: 27, 89, 144

Online databases: 37, 40
Order blank: 85

Page, copyright: 78
Page, dedication: 80
Page, epigraph: 80
Peer review: 94
Pen names: 78
Personal mission: 15
Photo sources: 106
Photographs: 93, 104
Pilot system: 87, 102
Play-on-words: 51
Preface: 81
Prestige: 119
Prevention books: 49
Price: 68
Printing: 101
Promises: 63
Promotion: 120, 136
Proofreading: 101
Pseudonyms: 78
Publisher: Chapters 9, 10
Publisher, finding: Chapter 10

Quotations: 94

Radio/TV: 19
Research: Chapter 3
Release, photo: 106

Rights: 135, 138
Risk comparison: 129
Rough draft: 89
Royalties: 134

Sales copy: 63
Self-publishing: 123
Selling hours: 16
Selling information: 17
Selling product: 16
Seminars: 20
Six musts: 28
Softcover: 13, 14
Software: Chapter 8
Special sales: 118, 136
Spine: 54
Stickers: 58
Strain, voice: 115
Subheads: 83
Subject selection: 27, 28
Subsidy press: 122
Subtitle: Chapter 4, 51
Success principles: 16

Table of contents: 80
Talk shows: 19
Territories: 134
Testimonials: 63-68, 77
Text: 82
Time required for writing: 103
Title: Chapter 4, 138
Title page: 78
Title placement: 57
Title testing: 52
Trim size: 74
Typesetting: 100

Vanity Press: 122
Via Voice: 112
Women, purchases by: 33
Working titles: 45, 50
Writer's block: 37, 102
Writing system: Chapter 7, 111
Writing v. Speaking: Chapter 8,
    89, 111

"Never trust anybody but yourself. That includes critics, friends and especially publishers."
—Mario Puzo

Quick Order Form

☎ **Fax orders:** (805) 968-1379. Send this form.

🖨 **Telephone orders:** Call 1(800) PARAPUB toll free, (727-2782). Have your credit card ready.

💻 **email orders**: orders@ParaPublishing.com.

🖥 **Postal orders:** Para Publishing, Dan Poynter, PO Box 8206-146, Santa Barbara, CA 93118-8206. USA. Telephone: (805) 968-7277

Please send the following Books, Discs or Reports. I understand that I may return any of them for a full refund—for any reason, no questions asked.

_____

_____

_____

Please send more FREE information on:
☐ Other books, ☐ Speaking/Seminars, ☐ Mailing lists, ☐ Consulting

Name: _____

Address: _____

City:_____ State: _____ Zip: _____ – _____

Telephone: _____

email address: _____

Sales tax: Please add 7.75% for products shipped to California addresses.

Shipping by air:
US: $4 for the first book or disk and $2.00 for each additional product.

International: $9 for 1st book or disk: $5 for each additional product (estimate).

Payment: ☐ Cheque, ☐ Credit card:

☐ Visa, ☐ MasterCard, ☐ Optima, ☐ AMEX, ☐ Discover

Card number: _____

Name on card: _____ Exp. date:_____ /_____

"Never trust anybody but yourself. That includes critics, friends and especially publishers."
—Mario Puzo

Quick Order Form

☎ **Fax orders:** (805) 968-1379. Send this form.

🖥 **Telephone orders:** Call 1(800) PARAPUB toll free, (727-2782). Have your credit card ready.

💻 **email orders:** orders@ParaPublishing.com.

🖥 **Postal orders:** Para Publishing, Dan Poynter, PO Box 8206-146, Santa Barbara, CA 93118-8206. USA. Telephone: (805) 968-7277

Please send the following Books, Discs or Reports. I understand that I may return any of them for a full refund—for any reason, no questions asked.

_____

_____

_____

Please send more FREE information on:
☐ Other books, ☐ Speaking/Seminars, ☐ Mailing lists, ☐ Consulting

Name: _____

Address: _____

City: _____ State: _____ Zip: _____ – _____

Telephone: _____

email address: _____

Sales tax: Please add 7.75% for products shipped to California addresses.

Shipping by air:
US: $4 for the first book or disk and $2.00 for each additional product.

International: $9 for 1st book or disk: $5 for each additional product (estimate).

Payment: ☐ Cheque, ☐ Credit card:

☐ Visa, ☐ MasterCard, ☐ Optima, ☐ AMEX, ☐ Discover

Card number: _____

Name on card: _____ Exp. date: _____ / _____